Metropolitan Open Space and Natural Process

Philadelphia metropolitan area from an altitude of 32,000 feet.

Metropolitan Open Space and Natural Process

DAVID A. WALLACE   ANN LOUISE STRONG
IAN L. McHARG   WILLIAM G. GRIGSBY
NOHAD A. TOULAN   WILLIAM H. ROBERTS

Edited by DAVID A. WALLACE

*Sponsored by The United States Department of
Housing and Urban Development, The State
of New Jersey, Department of Community
Affairs, The Commonwealth of
Pennsylvania, State Planning Board*

University of Pennsylvania · 1970 · Philadelphia

Library of Congress Catalog Card Number: 70-122385

The Urban Renewal Demonstration Project and the publication of this report were made possible through an Urban Renewal Demonstration Grant awarded by the Department of Housing and Urban Development, under the provisions of Sect. 314 of the Housing Act of 1954, as amended to the State of New Jersey, the Hon. William T. Cahill, Governor, and to the Commonwealth of Pennsylvania, the Hon. Raymond P. Shafer, Governor.

ISBN:0-8122-7617-5
Manufactured in the United States of America

Preface

The following is the report of a study conducted at the Institute for Environmental Studies of the Graduate School of Fine Arts of University of Pennsylvania.

Ian L. McHarg, Professor of Landscape Architecture and Regional Planning and Chairman of the Department of Landscape Architecture, was Principal Investigator. Dr. David A. Wallace, Professor of City Planning, was the Project Director.

Dr. William G. Grigsby, Professor of City Planning; William H. Roberts, Associate Professor of Landscape Architecture and Regional Planning; Ann Louise Strong, Professor of City and Regional Planning and Director of the Institute for Environmental Studies; Dr. Anthony R. Tomazinis, Associate Professor of City Planning; and Dr. Nohad A. Toulan, Urban Planning Director for the Greater Cairo Region, were the other participants in the study.

Dean William L. C. Wheaton, now at the University of California and formerly Professor of City Planning and Director of the Institute for Urban Studies, predecessor of the present Institute, was one of the initiators of the research and its first Project Director.

Acknowledgment is made of the contribution, through supervision and advice, of the staffs of the former Urban Renewal Administration (Howard Cayton, Frederick McLaughlin and Jack Underhill), New Jersey Department of Community Affairs (particularly Budd Chavooshian and Donald Stansfield), and of the Pennsylvania State Planning Board (notably Jesse Nalle and Mark Heyman). Substantial help has also been received from the planning directors of the five counties of the metropolitan area, namely Bucks, Chester,

Delaware, Montgomery, and the County and City of Philadelphia, acting with their staffs as a review committee.

Open space preservation around metropolitan areas is the central concern of the study. The authors maintain that if a wholesome natural environment is to be preserved while providing for amenable future development and if urban growth is to be guided in a logical sequence and direction, much land should remain open and in a natural state when urbanization occurs. The authors also propose that selection of areas to be kept open should be based on a "presumption for nature"—that is, that development should proceed where it least disrupts nature and vital natural processes. The areas most important to stable urban hydrology, we maintain, are the areas least suited to development, because development most disturbs the natural processes in those areas. An understanding of these natural processes and the role various kinds of land and water areas play in their balance and operation is therefore a vital necessity in planning future land use.

The study begins by identifying the most valuable natural resource areas in the Philadelphia SMSA.[1] The legal, economic, and design implications of protecting the natural functioning of these areas in close to their present state are then considered.

The design of the study also called for an analysis of the role which land retained in open space for resource, amenity, and design purposes could play in meeting regional recreation demand. In carrying out this task, Dr. Anthony R. Tomazinis developed a new method for estimating such demand. Dr. Tomazinis' work is being published separately because its scope differs considerably from the focus of the work presented here, all of which is directed to the central theme of metropolitan open space for natural resource functions.

D. A. W.

1. Philadelphia Standard Metropolitan Statistical Area (five counties).

Contents

Introduction by DAVID A. WALLACE   1

1. *Open Space from Natural Processes*   10
   IAN L. McHARG

2. *The Distribution and Value of Open Land in the
   Philadelphia Area*   53
   NOHAD A. TOULAN

3. *Incentives and Controls for Open Space*   81
   ANN LOUISE STRONG

4. *Economic and Fiscal Aspects of Open Space Preservation*   124
   WILLIAM G. GRIGSBY

5. *Design of Metropolitan Open Space Based on Natural
   Process*   148
   WILLIAM H. ROBERTS

Appendix   190
Referential Bibliography   197

Introduction

DAVID A. WALLACE

As metropolitan areas grow and megalopolis takes shape before our eyes, nearby open space where nature predominates seems doomed. Contact with nature—a constant delight to all ages—is harder and harder to come by. Forces apparently beyond our control, except in rare instances, eliminate all traces of an untouched countryside and replace it with thousands and thousands and thousands of houses. The pattern of ultimate suburban development finally removes the last vestige of woods, streams, thickets, and wildlife with the filling of vacant lots carelessly left over from the first great surge of growth. The individual houses that result are perhaps pleasant enough in the micro-scale. But unrelievedly continuous urbanization—even in the cases where the individual parts are attractive—appalls, bores, and numbs the senses.

Must it be this way? Or can there be a persuasive hypothesis which would support the protection of nature in the path of urbanization? We would hope so. Not only is the eye offended by the unending pattern of development, but the dollar cost in engineering construction to do nature's work when nature's defenses have been destroyed is high. What is to the developer's short-term benefit often becomes society's long-term cost. The right of an individual to build on and profit from any land, no matter what its natural resource functions and amenity value, has been and will be paid for manyfold by society in water shortages, pollution, floods, absence of beauty, and lack of recreation space. These externalities of site development are matters of increasing concern to all levels of government.

Government, however, to date seems largely impotent in dealing with the twin problems of urban sprawl and disappearing open space

FIG. 2. Suburban sprawl.

because the urban open space constituency has failed to master sufficient evidence to generate public sentiment for government intervention. The public losses from uncontrolled development and the potential gains through better alternatives must be demonstrated and the public educated to understand them. If the alternatives demand greater public intervention in the market process of land development, society must be convinced that the gains outweigh the loss of some freedom in the private use of land.

The following chapters suggest a new approach to metropolitan planning by those of us who have struggled with this problem of preserving open space as the urban fringe is developed.[1] A hypothesis is presented which favors nature over the market—a presumption for nature—and we explore the implications of that hypothesis. While we do not "prove" the hypothesis, in coming to grips with this problem we present sufficient evidence to add substantially to the arguments of those seeking positive open space action in the nation's urbanizing areas. A method is developed for incorporating the central concern for open space as part of the process of metropolitan planning.

THE PRESUMPTION FOR NATURE: DEVELOPMENT AS AN OPEN SPACE RESIDUAL

Ian McHarg initiated this new approach by challenging the normal practice of treating open space as the residual after economic and social needs of development were satisfied. He proposes simply to

1. The new approach is already becoming popular. Initiated by Ian McHarg and first published as part of a plan developed by his firm (Wallace, McHarg Associates), *Plan for the Valleys,* Green Spring and Worthington Valley Planning Council, Inc., was first published and widely distributed in 1963 and now is in its second printing. The new approach is advocated by the U.S. Department of the Interior to which Mr. McHarg has been an advisor. See S. B. Zisman *et al., Where Not To Build, a guide for open space planning,* Technical Bulletin 1, U.S. Department of the Interior, Bureau of Land Management, U.S. Government Printing Office, Washington, D.C., April 1968.

change the usual order of planning procedure and start with a presumption for nature; he suggests first identifying areas most important to natural processes. These should then strongly influence the pattern of development, particularly where land is plentiful and choice is possible.

In much metropolitan planning, a reverse procedure is followed. Desired or anticipated patterns of development result from "neatened up" normal growth plus concepts of how new growth ought to occur. These concepts range from the practical to abstract geometry and embrace garden cites to linear cities and metro-towns. The overall patterns are based on design, socio-economic, or movement concepts, with little if any concern for the natural environment. Open space becomes a residual and only accidentally may coincide with areas important to natural process.

McHarg's conviction is that development should generally occur where it will do as little damage as possible to the natural environment and specifically where it will upset the hydrologic cycle the least. After examining the elements of the ecosystem,[2] he chooses water in process as the best (most obvious and demonstrable) indicator of the extent to which urbanization is disturbing the preexisting balance of nature. He posits that urbanization on certain kinds of critical areas is particularly detrimental to water in process and from this proposition proceeds to a designation of three categories of open space. First are land or water areas most critical to the system which should be kept as open space in a natural state; second are areas which can stand limited development without major impact on natural processes; and, finally, there are the least critical areas whose development would not appear to affect significantly the natural processes.

McHarg places eight types of land or water in the first two cate-

2. See below, p. 19.

gories and describes the hydrologic functions of each. His presumption is that the burden of proof of the need for development of the critical areas should be weighed against the full evidence of their role in natural process.[3] And their development should be allowed to occur only when the external costs are properly levied against those bene-fitting from the development.

THE ECONOMIC, LEGAL, GOVERNMENTAL, AND DESIGN IMPLICATIONS OF THE PRESUMPTION FOR NATURE

Starting with seven of the eight types of land or water areas defined by McHarg—those whose urbanization is presumed to have greatest hydrologic significance—the other members of the study team have analyzed implications of protecting the hydrologic role of the land or water.[4]

Nohad Toulan sets the dimensions of the problem for the Philadelphia Standard Metropolitan Statistical Area (PSMSA). He examines the pattern of its urbanization and open land between 1930 and 1960. He estimates that in 1960, 1.8 million acres in the United States were still undeveloped out of a total 2.2 million acres. Toulan measures the open land and determines its spatial characteristics,

3. For further study of scientific evidence supporting the presumption for nature, see "The Plan and Program for the Brandywine," Institute for Environmental Studies, Philadelphia, Pa., November 1968. This is an attempt to establish a detailed hydrologic rationale for open space preservation.

4. Prime agricultural land was excluded as a type because it was so all pervasive, even though it undoubtedly plays a key hydrologic role, depending on its wise or unwise use. The U.S. Department of Agriculture has a vast literature concerning the application of agricultural technology to suburban problems. See Cecil H. Wadleigh, "The Application of Agricultural Technology," in *Soil, Water and Suburbia,* U.S. Department of Agriculture and U.S. Department of Housing and Urban Development, pp. 41–53, U.S. Government Printing Office 1968, and Marion Clawson "Land Use and Demand for Land in the United States," in *Modern Land Policy,* Land Economics Institute, 1960, pp. 12–14.

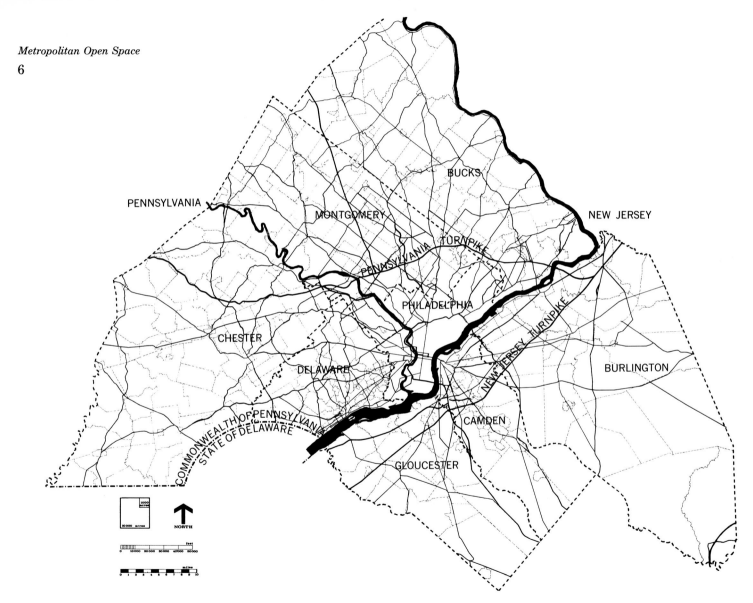

FIG. 3. Philadelphia Standard Metropolitan Statistical Area—1960 (showing states and counties).

ownership, and location. Through field studies he also calculates the market value of all open land in the PSMSA, as of 1962, its value by geographic location, and by location in one or more of six of McHarg's land types. The seventh, surface water was not measured separately by Toulan, but was included as part of adjacent land areas.

Ann Louise Strong examines ways to preserve the land (and water) critical to the system in a state compatible with its water resource functions. Measures range from outright public purchase to various forms of regulation, and include controls, incentives, and acquisition of development rights. She analyzes the legal, administrative, juris-dictional, and economic factors influencing a choice of method for preserving each of the classes of open space in a sufficiently unde-veloped state to protect the hydrologic functions in accord with the principles suggested. She proposes a method keyed to land value for selecting the method of land use control.

William G. Grigsby explores the problems of intervention in the suburban land market for open space preservation. Such preservation will cost a great deal of money, and has economic implications for land not controlled, for the pattern of development, and for the ultimate consumer. He examines the economic implications and the public fiscal costs with reference to the location of the land to be preserved, as well as with reference to distribution of the costs among units of government.

William H. Roberts presents an historical review of methods of open space delineation, as well as a survey of those currently in use in metropolitan planning. He observes that they pay attention to nature and natural process only incidentally, partially, and indirectly. Roberts goes on to outline in detail a procedure for including the new approach of the presumption for nature as an integral part of the metropolitan planning process. He examines a portion of the PSMSA to clarify design and development implications of McHarg's open space classifications. He concludes that the new approach, while *necessary* to the preservation of natural process, is by no means *sufficient* in itself to establish all open space requirements.

THE CONDUCT OF THE STUDY

As discussed above, this study presents a hypothesis of a presumption for nature in metropolitan planning. It identifies what kind of areas in the PSMSA are most critical to natural processes, locates and measures them, establishes principles as to their suitability (in some cases) for limited development and then examines the legal, economic and design implications of what has been described as a presumption for nature.

In order to carry out the empirical requirements of the study, an operational definition of open space in a specific geographic area was agreed on. Land in the Philadelphia SMSA was considered open space if empty and undeveloped or occupied by houses or other structures up to a density of one house per two acres (or its nonresidential equivalent).[5]

Private as well as public land was included in the definition. Major rivers were excluded from measurement even though they are important elements of open space. Minor streams, lakes, and other water courses were included as stated previously because in the actual measurement process exclusion was both impractical and unnecessary. Finally, the actual classification of the total open space in the Philadelphia SMSA by the natural characteristics selected did not discriminate below 16 acres because of difficulties of measurement.[6]

5. See Ann Louise Strong, *Open Space for Urban America,* Department of Housing and Urban Development, Washington, D.C., 1965 for detailed discussions of open space programs already underway in urban areas across the nation.

6. A grid system of 16 acres was superimposed on maps of the eight physiographic characteristics described below for the PSMSA. This grid was adjusted to the Penn-

We should make clear why the SMSA is used, for both open space far below the scale level of attention of this study[7] and open space beyond the boundaries of an SMSA are important. SMSA boundaries are after all selected for the decennial census and other fact gathering purposes, although they are somewhat arbitrary in location for the purposes of this study. Since they do include the already urbanized area and the open space in which the next twenty years or so of urbanization will take place, however, it is both convenient and appropriate to use them in this study.

While the classification of areas by their appropriateness for development is not new,[8] the approach presented here of a presumption for nature in the planning process is a new one. We have explored many of its implications while recognizing that much more evidence will be required before the hypothesis is substantiated and the method is widely operational. It is hoped that the work done here will contribute toward rational consideration and support of the role of open space in urban areas as part of the process of metropolitan planning.

Jersey Transportation Grid where coincident. When a characteristic filled one-half or more of the grid by visual measurement, the characteristic was recorded as occupying all of the grid. Where it occupied less than one-half, it was recorded as not occurring in the grid. A punch card was prepared for each grid containing these data along with land value and governmental unity. By testing it was found that in the aggregate the measurement technique averaged out with acceptable accuracy.

7. Zisman, *op. cit.,* p. 4 defines open space as "land or water surface open to the sky."

8. See for example Stuart F. Chapin, Jr., *Urban Land Use Planning* (Urbana: University of Illinois, 1965), pp. 300–303. The emphasis here as in other similar classifications is still primarily on a presumption for development. For an authoritative discussion of all aspects of land and land use classification, see Marion Clawson and Charles L. Stewart, *Land Use Information, A Critical Survey of U.S. Statistics Including Possibilities for Greater Uniformity.* Resources for the Future (Baltimore: Johns Hopkins University Press, 1965).

1

Open Space from Natural Processes

IAN L. McHARG

There is need for an objective and systematic method of identifying and evaluating land most suitable for metropolitan open space based on the natural roles that it performs. These roles can best be understood by examining the degree to which natural processes perform work for man without his intervention, and by studying the protection which is afforded and values which are derived when certain of these lands are undisturbed.

INTRODUCTION

Today a million acres of land each year are transformed from farmland and forest to hotdog stands and diners, gas stations, ranch and split-level homes, concrete and asphalt expanses, billboards and stretches of sagging wire, shopping centers, parking lots, and car cemeteries. There is little effective metropolitan planning and still less implementation of what is planned. Development occurs without reference to natural phenomena. Flood plains, marshes, steep slopes, woods, forests, and farmland are destroyed with little if any remorse; streams are culverted, ground water, surface water, and atmosphere polluted, floods and droughts exacerbated, and beauty superseded by vulgarity and ugliness. Yet the instinct for suburbia which has resulted in this enormous despoliation of nature is based upon a pervasive and profoundly felt need for a more natural environment.

The paradox and tragedy of metropolitan growth and suburbanization is that it destroys many of its own objectives. The open countryside is subject to uncontrolled, sporadic, uncoordinated, unplanned development, representing the sum of isolated short-term private decisions of little taste or skill. Nature recedes under this careless assault, to be replaced usually by growing islands of developments. These quickly coalesce into a mass of low-grade urban tissue, which eliminate all natural beauty and diminish excellence, both historic and modern. The opportunity for realizing an important part of the "American dream" continually recedes to a more distant area and a future generation. For this is the characteristic pattern of metropolitan growth. Those who escape from the city to the country are often encased with their disillusions in the enveloping suburb.

THE HYPOTHESIS

This pattern of indiscriminate metropolitan urbanization dramatizes the need for an objective and systematic way of identifying and preserving land most suitable for open space, diverting growth from it, and directing development to land more suitable for urbanization. The assumption is that not all land in an urban area needs to be, or even ever is, all developed. Therefore choice is possible. The discrimination which is sought would select lands for open space which perform important work in their natural condition, are relatively unsuitable for development, are self-maintaining in the ecological sense, and occur in a desirable pattern of interfusion with the urban fabric. The optimum result would be a system of two intertwining webs, one composed of developed land and the second consisting of open space in a natural or near natural state.

Heretofore, urbanization has been a positive act of transformation. Open space has played a passive role. Little if any value has been attributed to the natural processes often because of the failure to understand their roles and values. This is all the more remarkable when we consider the high land values associated with urban open space—Central Park in New York, Rittenhouse Square in Philadelphia being obvious examples. This lack of understanding has militated against the preservation or creation of metropolitan open space systems complementary to metropolitan growth. In this situation, governmental restraints are necessary to protect the public from the damaging consequences of private acts which incur both costs and losses to the public, when these acts violate and interrupt natural processes and diminish social values. There is an urgent need for land use regulations related to natural processes, based upon their intrinsic value and their permissiveness and limitations to development. This in turn requires general agreement as to the social values of natural process.

Planning that understands and properly values natural processes must start with the identification of the processes at work in nature. It must then determine the value of subprocesses to man, both in the parts and in the aggregate, and finally establish principles of development and nondevelopment based on the tolerance and intolerance of the natural processes to various aspects of urbanization. It is presumed that when the operation of these processes is understood, and land use policies reflect this understanding, it will be evidence that the processes can often be perpetuated at little cost.

The arguments for providing open space in the metropolitan region, usually dependent on amenity alone, can be substantially reinforced if policymakers understand and appreciate the operation of the major physical and biological processes at work. A structure for metropolitan growth can be combined with a network of open spaces that not only protects natural processes but also is of inestimable value for amenity and recreation.

In brief, it is hypothesized that the criteria for metropolitan open space should derive from an understanding of natural processes, their value to man, their permissiveness, and their prohibition to development. The method of physiographic analysis outlined here can lead to principles of land development and preservation for any metropolitan area. When applied as a part of the planning process, it can be a defensible basis for an open space system which goes far toward preserving the balance of natural processes and toward making our cities livable and beautiful.

Normal Metropolitan Growth Does Not Provide Open Space, Although Land Is Abundant

Without the use of such a method as described above, open space is infinitely vulnerable. An examination of the growth in this century of the major metropolitan areas of the United States demonstrates that urbanization develops primarily on open land rather than through redevelopment. The open space interspersed in areas of low-density development within the urban fabric is filled by more intensive uses and open space standards are lowered. Urban growth consumes open space both at the perimeter and within the urban fabric. The result is a scarcity of open space where population and demand are greatest. This phenomenon has aroused wide public concern as the growth of the cities, by accretion, has produced unattractive and unrelieved physical environments. Amenity, breathing space, recreational areas, and the opportunity for a contact with

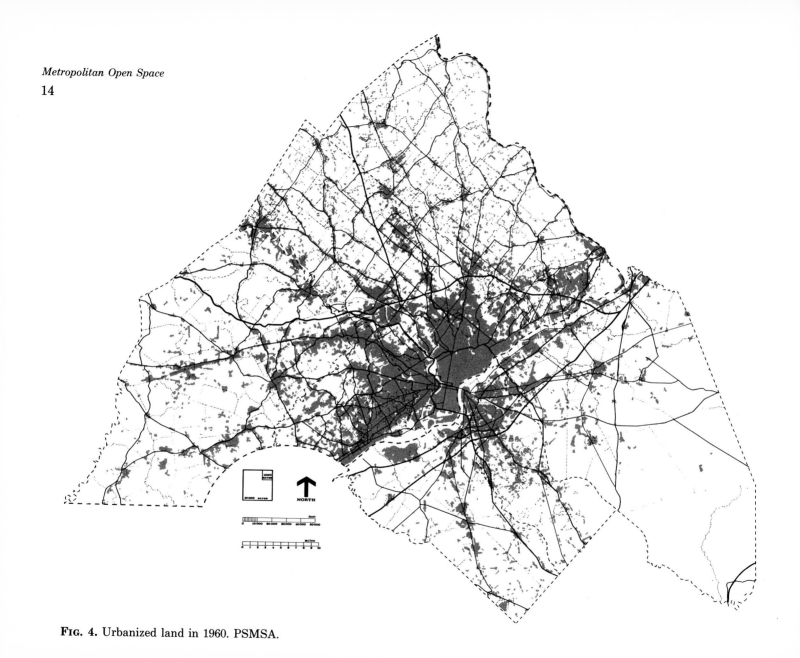

FIG. 4. Urbanized land in 1960. PSMSA.

nature for an expanding population are diminished. As important, it often exacerbates flood, drought, erosion, and humidity and it diminishes recreational opportunity, scenic, historic, and wildlife resources. Further, the absence of understanding of natural processes often leads to development in locations which are not propitious. When natural processes are interrupted, there are often resultant costs to society.

Demand for urban space is not only relatively but absolutely small. The 37 million inhabitants of megalopolis, constituting 24 per cent of the U. S. population, occupied 1.8 per cent of the land area of the continental United States.[1] Only five per cent of the United States is urbanized today; it is projected that less than ten per cent will be so utilized by the year 2000. Space is abundant. Even in metropolitan regions, where large urban populations exist in a semi-rural hinterland, the proportion of urban to rural land does not basically contradict the assertion of open space abundance. For example, in the Philadelphia SMSA, with 3, 500 square miles or 2,250,000 acres, only 19.1 per cent was urbanized in 1960. Here an increase in population from 4,000,000 to 6,000,000 is anticipated by 1980. Should this growth continue and occur at an average gross density of three families per acre, only 30 per cent of the land area would be in urban land use at that time. 2,300 square miles or 1,500,000 acres would still remain in open space.

The difficulty in planning lies in the relationship of this open space to urban uses. The market mechanism which raises the unit price of land for urban use tends to inhibit interfusion of open space in the urban fabric. Open space becomes normally a marginal or transitional use, remaining open only while land is awaiting development. The key question then is, if land is absolutely abundant, how can growth be

1. Jean Gottman, *Megalopolis* (New York: The Twentieth Century Fund, 1961), p. 26.

guided in such a way as to exploit this abundance for the maximum good?

Exceptions to the General Experience

While generally metropolitan growth has been unsympathetic to natural processes, there are exceptions. In the late nineteenth- and early twentieth-century park planning, water courses were an important basis for site selection. The Capper Cromptin Act selected river corridors in Washington, D.C. The Cook County Park System around Chicago consists of corridors of forests preponderantly based upon river valleys. The first metropolitan open space plan, developed for Boston by Charles Eliot in 1896, emphasized not only rivers, but also coastal islands, beaches and forested hills as site selection criteria. In 1928, Benton MacKaye, the originator of the Appalachian Trail, proposed using open space to control metropolitan growth in America, but did not base his open space on natural process.[2]

Sir Patrick Abercromby's Greater London Plan pays implicit attention to natural process in the location for the satellite towns, in the insistence on open space breaks between nucleated growth, in the recommendation that prime agricultural land should not be urbanized, and that river courses should constitute a basis for the open space system.

In recent studies conducted by Phillip Lewis on a state-wide basis for Illinois and Wisconsin,[3] physiographic determinants of land utilization have been carried beyond these earlier examples. Corridors have been identified which contain watercourses and their flood plains, steep slopes, forests, wildlife habitats and historic areas. These char-

2. Benton MacKaye, *The New Exploration: A Philosophy of Regional Planning* (New York: Harcourt Brace & Co., 1928).
3. E.g., State of Wisconsin, Dept. of Resource Development, *Recreation in Wisconsin,* The Department, 1962.

acteristics are of value to a wide range of potential supporters—conservationists, historians, and the like—and the studies demonstrate the coincidence of their interests in the corridors. The expectation is that these groups will coordinate their efforts and combine their influence to retain the corridors as open space. Resource development and preservation is advocated for them. In another recent study, ecological principles were developed and tested as part of a planning process for the Green Spring and Worthington valleys, northwest of Baltimore, Maryland.[4] Here the design process later described was evolved. Two more elaborate ecological studies, the first for Staten Island[5] and the second for the Twin Cities Metropolitan Region in Minnesota,[6] have undertaken to analyze natural processes to reveal intrinsic suitabilities for all prospective land uses. These are shown as unitary, complementary or in competition.

The present study of metropolitan open space is more general in its objective. It seeks to find the major structure of open space in the Philadelphia SMSA based upon the intrinsic values of certain selected natural processes to set the stage for the investigations described in the succeeding chapters.

Need for the Ecological Approach

There are, of course, several possible approaches. The first of these, beloved of the economist, views land as a commodity and allocates acres of land per thousand persons. In this view nature is seen as a

4. Wallace, McHarg Associates, *op. cit.* William G. Grigsby was Economic Consultant, Ann Louise Strong, Governmental and Legal Consultant, and William H. Roberts, Design Consultant in this first practical application of the new approach. (Wallace, McHarg Associates is now Wallace, McHarg, Roberts, and Todd).

5. Ian L. McHarg, "Processes as Values" in *Design with Nature* (New York: Natural History Press), 1969, pp. 103–115.

6. *An Ecological Study for the Twin Cities Metropolitan Region* (Wallace, McHarg, Roberts, and Todd, 1969), mimeo.

generally uniform commodity, appraised in terms of time-distance from consumers and the costs of acquisition and development. A second approach also falls within the orthodoxy of planning, and may be described as the geometrical method. Made popular by Sir Patrick Abercromby, the distinguished British planner, this consists of circumscribing a city with a green ring wherein green activities, agriculture, recreation, and the like, are preserved or introduced.

The ecological approach, however, would suggest quite a different method. Beginning from the proposition that nature is process and represents values, relative values would be ascribed to certain discernible processes. Then, operating upon the presumption that nature performs services for man without his intervention or effort, certain service-processes would be identified as social values. Yet further, recognizing that some natural processes are inhospitable to human use—floods, earthquakes, hurricanes—we would seem to discover intrinsic constraints or even prohibitions to man's use or to certain kinds of use.

Objective discussion between the ecologist and the economist would quickly reveal the fallacy of the commodity approach. Nature is by definition not a uniform commodity. In contrast, each and every area varies as a function of historical geology, climate, physiography, the water regimen, the pattern and distribution of soils, plants and animals. Each area will vary as process, as value and in the opportunities and constraints which it proffers or withholds from human use.

In a similiar discussion between ecologist and green belt advocate the question which most embarrasses the latter is whether nature is uniform within the belt and different beyond it. The next question is unlikely to receive an affirmative answer, "Does nature perform particular roles within the belt to permit its definition?" Clearly the ecologist emerges a victor in these small skirmishes, but now the burden is upon him. What is the ecological approach to the selections of metropolitan open space?

There is, at present, no existing ecological model[7] for a city or metropolitan region; it is necessary, therefore, to embark upon a theoretical analysis of natural process without the aid of such a model.

Plant and animal communities require solar energy, food, nutrients, water, and protection from climate extremes, and shelter. These conditions must be substantially regular in their provision. In order to ensure these optimal conditions, nonhuman or primitive-human systems have adapted to the natural environment and its constituent organisms to ensure a complex process of energy utilization, based upon photosynthesis, descending through many food chains to final decomposition and nutrient recirculation. In response to the problem of climatic extremes these communities do modify the microclimate. Such natural systems have mechanisms whereby water movement is modified to perform the maximum work. The aggregate of these processes is a stable, complex ecosystem in which entropy is low and energy is conserved.[8]

The net result is a system with high energy utilization and production, continuous soil formation, natural defenses against epidemic disease, microclimatic extremes diminished, minimal oscillation between flood and drought, minor erosion, and natural water purification. There obviously are many advantages which accrue to civilized man from this condition—a viable agriculture and forestry, abundant fish and wildlife, natural water purification, stability in the water system, defense against flood and drought, diminished erosion, sedimentation and silting, and a self-cleaning environment with high recreational potential and amenity.

7. Ecological model is a theoretical construct, either descriptive or mathematical, by which the energy flow of an organic system can be described.

8. See E. P. Odum, *The Fundamentals of Ecology* (Philadelphia: W. B. Saunders, 1959), Chapter 3.

The values of the natural processes far exceed the values which usually are attributed to them. Agriculture, forestry, and fisheries are taken into consideration in the evaluation of regional assets, but atmospheric oxygen, amelioration of climate and microclimate, water evaporation, precipitation, drainage or the creation of soils tend to be disregarded. Yet the composite picture of the region's resources must include all natural processes. Beginning with the values of agriculture, forestry, and fisheries, the value of minerals and the value of the land for education, recreation, and amenity may be added. Agricultural land has an amenity which is not generally attributed, since it is also a landscape which is maintained as a byproduct. Forests equally have an amenity value and are self-cleaning environments, requiring little or no maintainance.

Water has values which transcend those related to certain discrete aspects of the hydrologic cycle. In this latter category are many important processes—water in agriculture, industry, commerce, recreation, education and amenity, consumption, cooling, hydroelectric generation, navigation, water transport and dilution, waste reduction, fisheries, and water recreation.

Value is seldom attributed to the atmosphere; yet the protection from lethal cosmic rays, insulation, the abundance of oxygen for animal metabolism and the carbon dioxide for plant metabolism which it affords, all demonstrate an indispensability equal to land and water. In terms of positive attributed value the atmosphere has been accorded virtually none. Only when atmosphere has become polluted is the cost and necessity of ensuring clean air recognized.

Even in the exceptional condition when natural processes are attributed value as in agriculture and forestry, these are generally held in such low esteem that they can not endure in the face of competition from urban or industrial uses. It is impossible to construct a value system which includes the vast processes described. It is, however, quite possible to recognize the fundamental value of these processes, their characteristics, and their relationship to industrial and urban processes. This understanding should lead to a presumption in favor of nature rather than the prevailing disdain.

Working toward the goal of developing working principles for land use planning in general and the selection of metropolitan open space in particular, it is advantageous to examine the degree to which natural processes perform work for man without his intervention and the protection achieved by leaving certain sub-processes in their natural state without development. While this cannot yet be demonstrated quantitatively, it can be described.

Natural processes which perform work for man include water purification, atmospheric pollution dispersal, microclimate amelioration, water storage and equalization, flood control, erosion control, topsoil accumulation, and the ensurance of wildlife populations.

Areas which are subject to volcanic action, earthquakes, tidal waves, tornadoes, hurricanes, floods, drought, forest fires, avalanches, mud slides, and subsidence, should be left undeveloped in order to avoid loss of life and property. In addition, there are other areas which are particularly vulnerable to human intervention; this category includes beach dunes, major animal habitats, breeding grounds, spawning grounds, and water catchment areas. There are also areas of unusual scenic, geological, biological, ecological, and historic importance. In each of these cases it is apparent that wise land use planning should recognize natural processes and respond to them. As many of these processes are water related, it would seem that water may be a useful indicator of these major physical and biological processes described as natural processes.

Water and Natural Processes

Water, as the agent of erosion and sedimentation, is linked with geological evolution to the realities of physiography. Mountains, hills, valleys, and plains which result, experience variety of climate and microclimate consequent upon their physiography. The combination of physiography and climate determines the incidence and distribution of plants and animals, their niches and habitats.

The use of water as a unifying concept links marsh and forest, rivers and clouds, ground and surface water, all as interdependent aspects of a single process. It permits us to see that the marsh filled in the estuary and the upland forest felled are comparable in their effect, that pollution to surface water may affect distant ground water, that building of an outlying suburb may affect the flood height in the city. Although we lack an ecological model, a gross perception of natural process may be revealed through the selection of water as a unifying process. This may suggest land use policies reflecting the permissiveness and prohibitions of the constituent phases of water in process. By this useful method the constituent roles of open space may be seen and the optimal distribution of open space in the metropolitan region may be discerned.

Water is not the best indicator or theoretical tool for ecological planning. The physiographic region is perhaps the best unit for ecological studies since there tends to be a marked consistency within each physiographic region and distinct variations between them.

WATER AND THE ROLES OF MAJOR PHYSIOGRAPHIC REGIONS

In this study the roles of the physiographic regions have been simplified to three components: the first, the Uplands of the Piedmont and second, the remainder of that region with the final category being the Coastal Plain. The area to be studied is the Philadelphia Standard Metropolitan Statistical Area, three and one-half thousand square miles which constitute the metropolitan region and straddle Coastal Plain and Piedmont, a situation typical of many cities on the eastern seaboard.

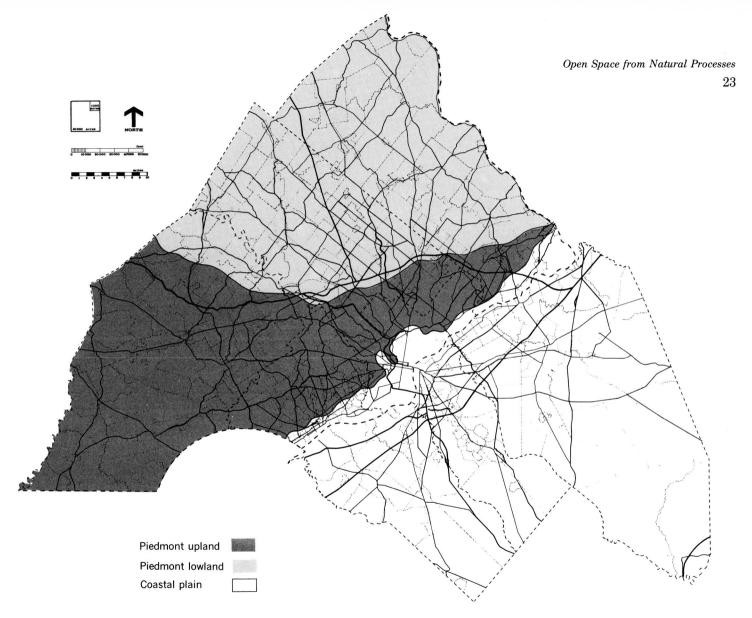

FIG. 5. Piedmont upland, lowland, and Coastal Plain. PSMSA.

The Uplands

The Uplands are the hills of the watershed, the highest elevations, wherein many streams begin, their watercourses narrow, steep, and rocky. The soils tend to be thin and infertile from long term erosion. In the Philadelphia metropolis, the Uplands consist of a broad band of low hills, 12 to 20 miles wide, bending northeast-southwest obliquely through the area. As a result of the absence of glaciation in this area the rivers and streams lack natural impoundments and are, therefore, particularly susceptible to seasonal fluctuations.

The natural restraints to flooding and drought, contributing to equilibrium, are mainly the presence and distribution of vegetation, principally forests and their soils, particularly on the uplands and their steep slopes. Vegetation absorbs and utilizes considerable quantities of water. In fact, vegetation and their soils act as a sponge restraining extreme runoff, releasing water slowly over longer periods, diminishing erosion and sedimentation—in short, diminishing the frequency and intensity of oscillation between flood and drought and operating towards equilibrium.

In the Uplands, land use policies should protect and enhance forests and other vegetative cover to diminish runoff, oscillation between flood and drought, and the insurance of natural water purification. On steep slopes, land use management would notably include forestation programs. Land uses should then be related to permissiveness and prohibitions inherent in such a region related to the primary role of the Upland sponge in the water economy.

The Piedmont

The Piedmont is also nonglaciated in the study area, and consists of the gentler slope below the Uplands. It sustains fertile soils which, in limestone areas, are equal in fertility to the richest in the entire

United States. In the three divisions it is in the Piedmont alone that fertile soils abound. Unglaciated, the Piedmont, like the Uplands, lacks natural impoundment and is flood prone.

Here is the land most often developed for agriculture. These lands too, tend to be favored locations for villages, towns, and cities. Here, forests are often residues or the products of regeneration on abandoned farms. Steep slopes in the Piedmont are associated with the dissected banks of streams and rivers.

The agricultural Piedmont does not control its own defenses. It is either affected by or defended from flood and drought by the conditions in the Uplands and Coastal Plain. When cropland is ploughed and lacks vegetation, when building sites are bared, they are subject to erosion and contribute to sediment yield. Even when covered with growing crops, the average runoff here exceeds the forest. Nonetheless, the vegetative cover, configuration, and conservation practices in the agricultural Piedmont can either increase or diminish flood and drought. The Piedmont is particularly vulnerable to both. The presence of forests and woodlands will act as ameliorative agents as they do in the Uplands and the presence of vegetation will diminish runoff by absorption, friction, and through increased percolation.

The fine capillary streams of the Uplands become the larger streams and rivers of the Piedmont, and their volume increases proportionately, as does their flood potential and their oscillation to low flow.

In the Piedmont, fertile soils should be perpetuated as an irreplaceable resource. Both agriculture and urbanization are primary contributors to erosion and sedimentation; they are also the major contributors to water pollution from pesticides, fertilizers, domestic and industrial wastes.

Planning should relate water pollution to specific stream capacities; withdrawals of water to specific capacities of surface and ground water; conservation practices to erosion control for farmland and construction sites.

The Coastal Plain

The Coastal Plain has been, through much of geologic time, a vast depository of sediments eroded from the Uplands. The soils are shallow and acid, overlaying sedimentary material. These are naturally infertile although in New Jersey such sandy soils with abundant fertilizer and water, support extensive truck farming.

The major physiographic characteristics of the Coastal Plain are its flatness, the poverty of its soils, the abundant marshes, bays, estuaries, the unique flora of the pine barrens, and finally, the great resources of ground water in aquifers.

The incidence of flood and drought in the Piedmont and Coastal Plains are not only consequent upon the upland sponge, but also upon estuarine marshes, particularly where these are tidal. Here, at the mouth of the watershed, at the confluence of important rivers or river and sea, the flood components of confluent streams or the tidal components of flood assumes great importance. In the Philadelphia metropolitan area the estuary and the ocean are of prime importance as factors in flood.

A condition of intense precipitation over the region combined with high tides, full estuary and strong on-shore winds bring together the elements that portend floods. The estuarine marshes and their vegetation constitute the major defense against this threat. These areas act as enormous storage reservoirs, absorbing mile-feet of potentially destructive waters, thus reducing flood potential. This function may be described as the estuarine sponge, in contrast to the Upland sponge. The water resources of these aquifers represent a significant economic value.

In the Coastal Plain, the susceptibility to flood of these areas and the invaluable role of marshlands as flood storage reservoirs should also be reflected in land use policies which could ensure the perpetuation of their natural role in the water economy. The value of ground water in aquifers should be reflected in land use policy.

Finally, the extensive forests of the pine barrens and their unique flora depend upon fire, which is an inevitable and recurrent threat. Here extensive urbanization makes such a threat actuality: pine barrens are not suitable sites for development.

These three major divisions are clearly different in their permissiveness and prohibition, their roles in the water regimen: the Uplands should be viewed and planned as the upstream control area for water processes, flood, drought, water quality, erosion control, and an area of high recreational potential. This region is not normally selected for extensive urbanization and can be easily protected from it. But it performs its role best when extensively forested.

The Coastal Plain performs a primary flood control, water supply and water related recreation function, and is not suited to extensive urbanization. The entire region, characterized by rivers, marshes, bays, and estuaries is critical to wildlife. Properly used, it offers a great recreational potential. In contrast, the Piedmont, with the exception of prime agricultural areas, is tolerant to urbanization. Although the prime farmland of this region is an irreplaceable resource, a scenic value, and requires defense against urbanization, the Piedmont should be the region for major urban growth in the future.

Planning for natural processes at this scale would regulate urban development in Uplands and Coastal Plain, concentrate it in the Piedmont, on nonprime agricultural land. Connecting these regions would be an undeveloped fabric of streams, rivers, marshes, bays and estuaries, the steep slopes of dissected watercourses, as water corridors permeating the entire metropolis.

SIGNIFICANT PHYSIOGRAPHIC PHENOMENA AND THEIR ROLES

The major physiographic divisions reveal the principal roles in the water regimen and should constitute an important generalized basis for identification of natural processes and planning. Yet it is necessary to have a greater specificity as to the constituent roles of natural process. Toward this end, eight components have been selected for identification and examination. It is clear that they are to some extent identifiable and perform discrete roles. These eight constituent phenomena are:

1. Surface Water
2. Flood Plains

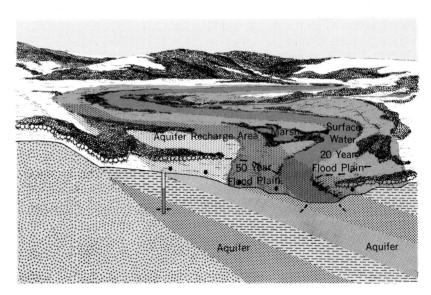

FIG. 6. Water features.

3. Marshes
4. Aquifers
5. Aquifer Recharge Areas
6. Steep Slopes
7. Forests and Woodlands
8. Prime Agricultural Land

The first five have a direct relationship to water; the remaining three are water-related in that they either have been determined by, or are determinants of water-in-process.

This group of water-related parameters is selected as containing the most useful indicators of natural process for a majority of metro-

FIG. 7. Land features.

politan regions in the United States. They appear to be the most productive for the project area under study, but the underlying hypothesis of natural process would take precedence in these areas where other parameters prove to be more illuminating. That is, the selection of criteria for a system of metropolitan open space can best be developed from an understanding of the major physical and biological process *of the region itself.* The interconnected phenomena should be integrated into a unified system to which the planning process responds.

Varying Permissiveness to Urban Uses

Having identified certain sub-processes, it is necessary to describe their instrinsic function and value and then to determine the degree to which the performance of natural process is prohibitive or permissive to other land uses.

The terms prohibitive and permissive are used relatively. In no case does natural process absolutely prohibit development. Yet in a condition of land abundance, there is available a choice as to location of development. This being so, areas of importance to natural process should not be selected where alternative locations of lesser importance are available. Further, development of natural process areas should occur only where supervening benefits result from such development, in excess of those provided by natural process. Still further, the tolerances of natural processes to development by type, amount, and location are an important constituent of land use policy.

Surface Water (5,671 linear miles)[9]

In a situation of land abundance, restraints should be exercised on the development of surface water and riparian land. In principle,

9. 5,671 linear miles in the PSMSA; surface water has been identified as all permanent streams shown on U.S.G.S. 1:24,000 Series. This estimate and those which followed are explained in Chapter III.

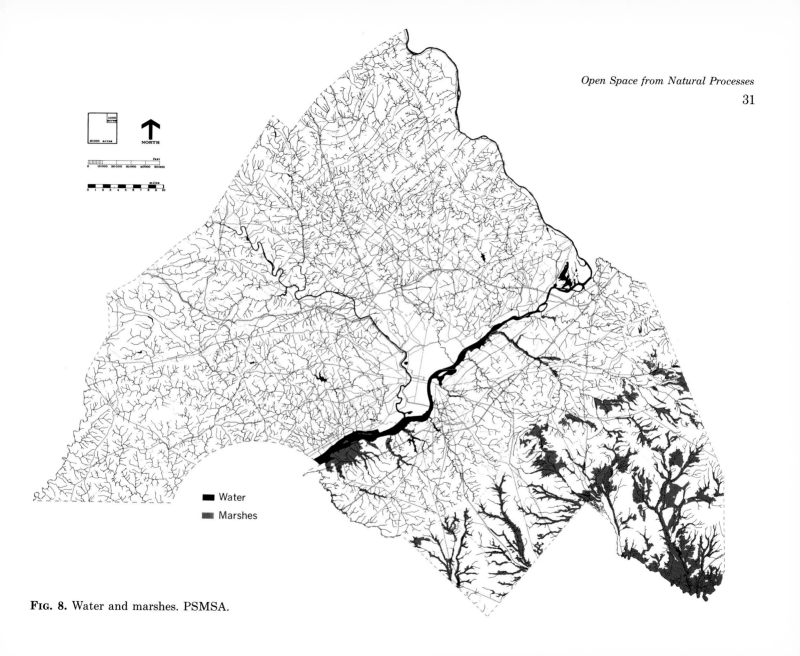

■ Water
▨ Marshes

FIG. 8. Water and marshes. PSMSA.

only those land uses which are inseparable from waterfront locations should occupy riparian lands; land uses thereon should be limited to those which do not diminish the present or prospective value of surface water or stream banks for water supply, amenity, or recreation.

In the category of consonant land uses would fall port and harbor facilities, marinas, water treatment plants, sewage treatment plants, water related industry, and in certain instances, water-using industries.

In the category of land uses which need not diminish existing or prospective value of surface water would fall agriculture, forestry, institutional open space, recreational facilities, and, under certain conditions, open space for housing.

In the category of land uses which would be specifically excluded would be industries producing toxic or noxious liquid effluents, waste dumps, nonwater-related industry or commerce.

The presumption is then that surface water as a resource best performs its function in a natural state and that land uses which do not affect this state may occupy riparian land, but other functions be permitted according to the degree which their function is indivisibly water related.

Marshes (133,984 acres; 7.44 per cent)

In principle, land use policy for marshes should reflect the roles of flood and water storage, wildlife habitat, and fish spawning grounds. Land uses which do not diminish the operation of the primary roles are compatible. Thus, hunting, fishing, sailing, recreation, in general, would be permissible. Certain types of agriculture, notably cranberry bogs, would also be compatible. Isolated urban development might also be permitted if the water storage role of marshes were not diminished by the filling and accelerated runoff that such development would entail.

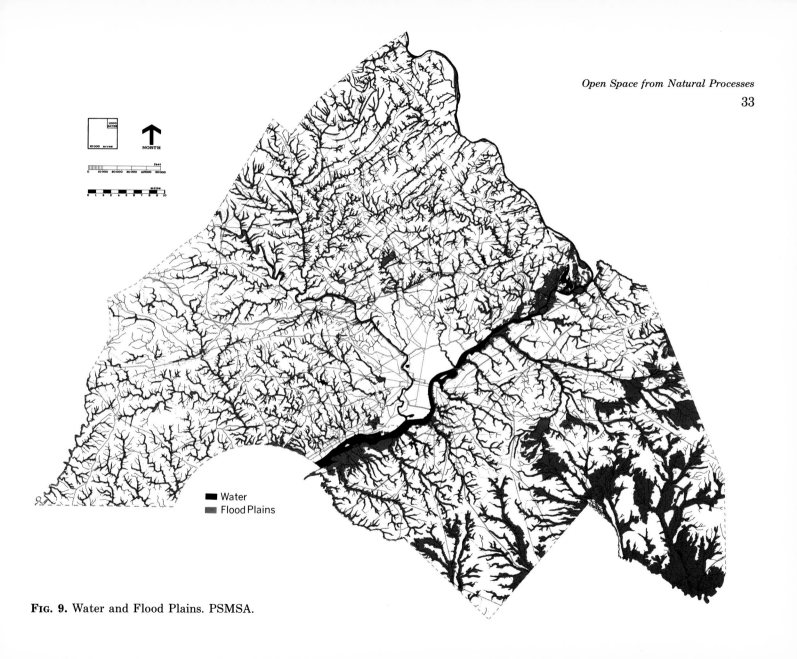

Water
Flood Plains

Fig. 9. Water and Flood Plains. PSMSA.

Flood Plains (339,760 acres; 18.86 per cent)

The Flood Plain parameter must be attributed a particular importance because of its relation to loss of life and property damage. The best records seem to indicate that the incidence and intensity of flooding in metropolitan areas is on the increase.[10] The presumption is that this results from the reduction of forest and agricultural land, erosion and sedimentation, and the urbanization of watersheds. This being so, there is every reason to formulate a land utilization policy for flood plains related to safeguarding of life and property.[11]

The incidence of floods may be described as recorded maxima. For the Delaware River, the maximum recorded floods are those of 1950 and 1955. The alternate method of flood description relates levels of inundation to cyclical storms and describes these as flood levels of anticipated frequency or probability.

There is, then, a conflict of use for this land between water and other types of occupancy. This conflict is most severe in areas of frequent flooding which, however, occupy the smallest flood plain. The conflict diminishes in frequency with the more severe floods, which occupy the largest flood plain. It would seem possible to relate the utilization of the flood plain to the incidence and severity of cyclical flooding.[12]

10. S. W. Witala, *Some Aspects of the Effect of Urban and Suburban Development on Runoff* (Lansing, Michigan: U.S. Department of the Interior, Geological Survey), August, 1961.

11. C. Kates, Robert William, and Gilbert F. White, "Flood Hazard Evaluation," in *Papers on Flood Problems,* Gilbert F. White, ed., University of Chicago, Dept. of Geography, Research Paper No. 70, suggest classification of flood zones into prohibitive, restrictive, and warning zones, based on physiographic analysis. The prohibitive zone would protect structures and fill to preserve the channel capacity in flood conditions; the restrictive zone would simply alert users they were within the flood plain and the decision to accomodate would be theirs.

12. See C. Kates and Robert William, *Hazard and Choice Perception in Flood Plain Management,* University of Chicago, Department of Geography, Research Paper No.

Increasingly, the 50 year or 2 per cent probability flood plain is being accepted as that area from which all development should be excluded save those functions which are either benefited or unharmed by flooding or those land uses which are inseparable from flood plains.

Thus, in principle, only such land uses which are either improved or unharmed by flooding should be permitted to occupy the 50 year flood plain. In the former category fall agriculture,[13] forestry, recreation, institutional open space, and open space for housing. In the category of land uses inseparable from flood plains are ports and harbors, marinas, water related industry, and under certain circumstances, water using industry.

Aquifers (149,455 acres; 8.3 per cent)

The definition of an aquifer as a water bearing stratum of rock, gravel or sand is so general that enormous areas of land could be so described. For any region the value of an aquifer will relate to the abundance or poverty of water resources. In the Philadelphia area the great deposits of porous material parallel to the Delaware River are immediately distinguishable from all other aquifers in the region by their extent and capacity.

Aquifers may vary from ground water resources of small quantity to enormous underground resources. They are normally measured by yields of wells or by the height of the water table. The aquifer in New Jersey parallel to the Delaware River has been estimated by the Soil Conservation Service to have a potential capacity of one billion gallons

---

78, 1962, for thorough discussion of the conditions and value judgments concerning occupancy of flood plains. It is evident from this analysis that flood controls are most easily established where the certainty of flood occurrence is high.

13. See Ian Burton, *Types of Agricultural Occupancy of Flood Plains in the U. S. A.,* University of Chicago, Dept. of Geography, Research Paper No. 75, 1962, for a more detailed consideration of agricultural occupancy of flood plains.

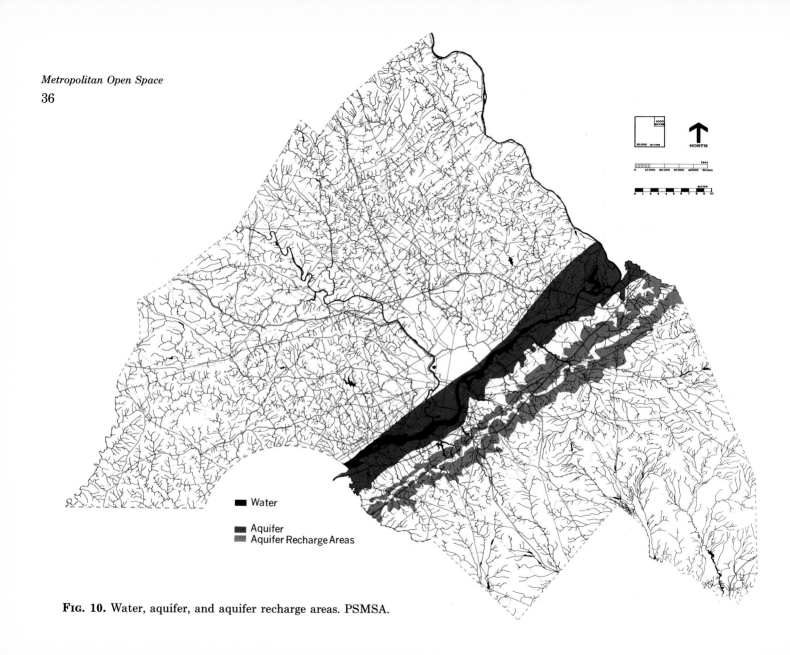

FIG. 10. Water, aquifer, and aquifer recharge areas. PSMSA.

per day. This valuable resource requires restraints upon development of the surface to insure quality and quantity of aquifer resources. Consequently, development using septic tanks and industries disposing toxic or noxious effluents should be regulated. Injection wells should be expressly prohibited. The matter of surface percolation is also important, and as percolation will be greatest from permeable surfaces. there are good reasons for maximizing development at the extremes of density—either sewered high density development or very low density free standing houses. Land use policy for aquifers is less amenable to generalized recommendation than the remaining categories, as aquifers vary with respect to capacity, yield, and susceptibility. Consequently, there will be ranges of permissiveness attributable to specific aquifers as a function of their role and character.

In principle, no land uses should be permitted above an aquifer which inhibit the primary role as water supply and reservoir regulating oscillations between flood and drought.

Agriculture, forestry, and recreation clearly do not imperil aquifers. Industries, commercial activities, and housing, served by sewers, are permissible up to limits set by percolation requirements. Sources of pollutants or toxic material, and extensive land uses which reduce soil permeability, should be restricted or prohibited.

Aquifer Recharge Areas (83,085 acres; 4.61 per cent)

Such areas are defined as points of interchange between surface and ground water. In any water system certain points of interchange will be critical; in the Philadelphia metropolitan area the interchange between the Delaware River, its tributaries and the parallel aquifer, represents the recharge area which is most important and which can be clearly isolated. Percolation is likely to be an important aspect of recharge. Thus, two considerations arise: the location of surface to ground water interchange below the ground, and percolation of surface to ground water.

By careful separation of polluted river water from the aquifer and by the impounding of streams transecting the major aquifer recharge areas, the aquifer can be managed and artificially recharged. Ground water resources can be impaired by extensive development which waterproofs the surfaces, by development which occupies desirable impoundments valuable for aquifer management and by pollution.

In principle all proposed development on aquifer recharge areas should be measured against the likely effect upon recharge. Injection wells, disposal of toxic or offensive materials should be forbidden, channel widening, deepening and dredging should be examined for their effect upon recharge as should deep excavations for trunk sewers. Surface development and sewage disposal on such an area should be limited by considerations of percolation.

Prime Agricultural Land (248,816 acres; 11.7 per cent)

Prime agricultural soils represent the highest level of agricultural productivity; they are uniquely suitable for intensive cultivation with no conservation hazards. It is extremely difficult to defend agricultural lands when their cash value can be multiplied tenfold by employment for relatively cheap housing. Yet, the farm is the basic factory, the farmer is the country's best landscape gardener and maintenance work force, the custodian of much scenic beauty. Utilization of farmland by urbanization is often justifiable as the highest and best use of land at current land values, yet the range of market values of farmlands does not reflect the long term value or the irreplaceable nature of these living soils. An omnibus protection of all farmland is indefensible; protection of the best soils in a metropolitan area would appear not only defensible, but clearly desirable.

Jean Gottman has recommended that "the very good soils are not extensive enough in Megalopolis to be wastefully abandoned to non-agricultural uses." [14] The soils so identified are identical to the prime agricultural soils in the metropolitan area.

While farmland is extremely suitable for development and such lands can appreciate in value by utilization for housing, it is seldom considered that there is a cost involved in the development of new farmland. The farmer, displaced from excellent soils by urbanization, often moves to another site on inferior soils. Excellent soils lost to agriculture for building can finally only be replaced by bringing inferior soils into production. This requires capital investment. "Land that is not considered cropland today will become cropland tomorrow, but at the price of much investment." [15]

In the Philadelphia SMSA by 1980 only 30 per cent of the land area will be urbanized; 70 per cent will remain open. Prime agricultural lands represent only 11.7 per cent of the area. Therefore, given a choice, prime soils should not be developed.

In principal, U.S.D.A. Category 1, soils, are recommended to be exempted from development (save by those functions which do not diminish their present or prospective productive potential). This would suggest retirement of prime soils into forest, utilization as open space for institutions, for recreation or in development for housing at densities no higher than one house per 25 acres.

Steep Lands (262,064 acres; 14.55 per cent)

Steep lands and the ridges which they constitute are central to the problems of flood control and erosion. Slopes in excess of 12° are not recommended for cultivation by the Soil Conservation Service. The same source suggests that for reasons of erosion, these lands are

14. Gottman, *op. cit.,* p. 95.
15. Edward Higbee, Chapter 6, p. 326.

Steep Slopes
Prime Agricultural Land

Fig. 11. Steep slopes and prime agricultural land. PSMSA.

unsuitable for development. The recommendations of the Soil Conservation Service are that steep slopes should be in forest and that
cultivation of such slopes be abandoned.

In relation to its role in the water regimen, steepness is a matter
not only of degree, but of vegetation and porosity. Two ranges of slopes
are identified in our study of the PSMSA: 15 to 25 per cent, and
greater than 25 per cent. The first category of 15 per cent is identified
as those slopes for which major site-engineering begins to be necessary
to accommodate development. Roads should be equally parallel to
the slope rather than perpendicular. Coverage by houses and roads
should be compensated by measures to slow down runoff. Examination
of a number of examples suggests 15 per cent as the danger point for
any development at all, but further empiric research is necessary.
Above 25 per cent, however, there appears widespread agreement that
no development should occur and land should be treated to decrease
runoff as much as possible.[16]

In summary, erosion control and diminution of velocity of runoff
are the principal water problems of steep slopes. Land uses compatible
with minimizing these problems would be mainly forestry, recreation,
and low-density development on the less-steep slopes. Since such
slopes also tend to dominate landscapes, their planting in forests
would provide great amenity.

Forests and Woodlands (588,816 acres; 32.7 per cent)

The natural vegetative cover for most of this region is forest. Where
present, this exerts an ameliorative effect upon microclimate; it exercises a major balancing effect upon the water regimen, diminishing
erosion, sedimentation, flood and drought. The scenic role of wood-

16. E.g., in Pittsburgh, 25 per cent and greater slopes are now subject to an ordinance
prohibiting further development.

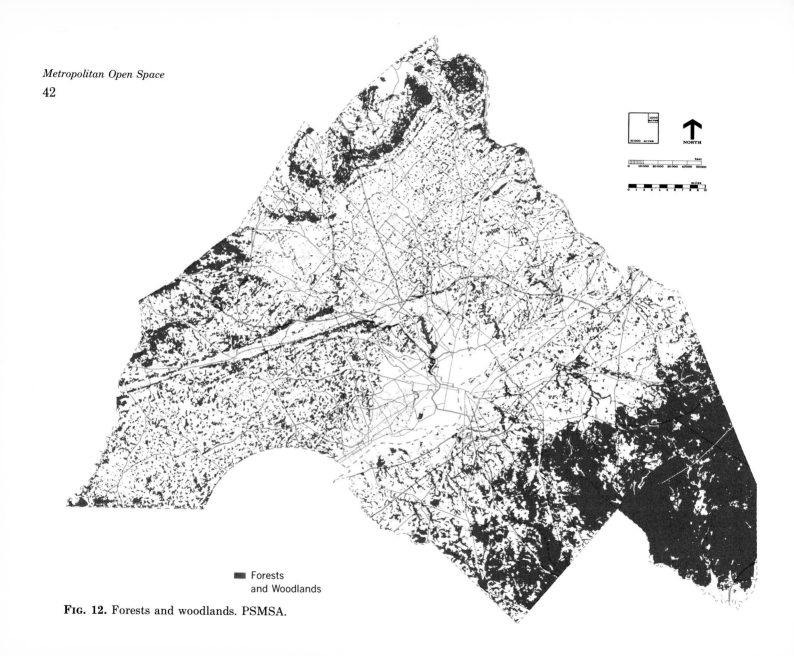

Forests
and Woodlands

FIG. 12. Forests and woodlands. PSMSA.

lands is apparent as is the provision of a habitat for game. The recreational potential of forests is among the highest of all categories. In addition, the forest is a low maintenance, self-perpetuating landscape, a resource in which accrual of timber inventory is continuous.

Forests can be employed for timber production, water management, wildlife habitats, as air sheds, recreation, or for any combination of these uses. In addition, forests can absorb development in concentrations which will be determined by the demands of natural process which they are required to satisfy. Where scenic considerations alone are operative, mature forests could absorb housing up to a density of one house per acre without loss of their forest aspect.

TABLE 1.

Limited Development Areas	Recommended Land Uses
1. Surface Water and Riparian Lands	Ports, harbors, marinas, water treatment plants, water related industry, open space for institutional and housing use, agriculture, forestry and recreation.
2. Marshes	Recreation.
3. 50 Year Flood Plains	Ports, harbors, marinas, water treatment plants, water related and water using industry, agriculture, forestry, recreation, institutional open space, open space of housing.
4. Aquifers	Agriculture, forestry, recreation, industries which do not produce toxic or offensive effluents. All land uses within limits set by percolation.
5. Aquifer Recharge Areas	As aquifers.
6. Prime Agricultural Lands	Agriculture, forestry, recreation, open space for institutions, housing at 1 house per 25 acres.
7. Steep Lands	Forestry, recreation, housing at maximum density of 1 house per 3 acres, where wooded.
8. Forests and Woodlands	Forestry, recreation, housing at densities not higher than 1 house per acre.

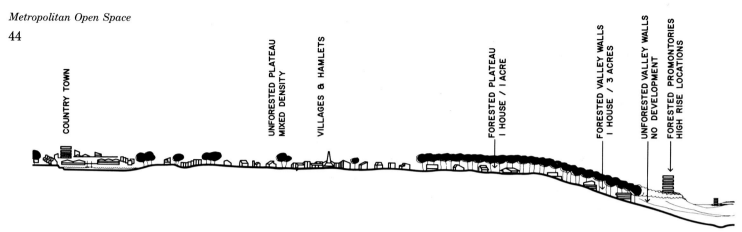

COUNTRY TOWN

UNFORESTED PLATEAU
MIXED DENSITY

VILLAGES & HAMLETS

FORESTED PLATEAU
1 HOUSE / 1 ACRE

FORESTED VALLEY WALLS
1 HOUSE / 3 ACRES

UNFORESTED VALLEY WALLS
NO DEVELOPMENT

FORESTED PROMONTORIES
HIGH RISE LOCATIONS

FIG. 13. Physiographic determinants of form

Land uses for forests should be determined by the natural process roles which the forest is required to play in the water regimen.

OPEN SPACE AND AIRSHEDS

The atmosphere of a metropolitan area has a capacity to diffuse air pollution based upon temperature, air composition, and movement. Concentration of pollution is associated with cities and industries, replacement of polluted air and its diffusion depends upon air movements over pollution free areas. These will be related to wind movements, and must be substantially free of pollution sources if relief is to be afforded to air pollution over cities. One can use the analogy of the watershed and describe the pollution free areas, tributory to the city, as the airsheds.

The central phase of air pollution is linked to temperature inversion during which the air near the ground does not rise to be replaced by in-moving air. Under inversion, characterized by clear nights with little wind, the earth is cooled by long wave radiation and the air near the ground is cooled by the ground. During such temperature inversions with stable surface air layers, air movement is limited; in cities, pollution becomes increasingly concentrated. In Philadelphia "significant" inversions occur one night in three. Parallel and related to inversion is the incidence of "high" pollution levels, which occurred on twenty-four "episodes" from 2 to 5 days in duration between 1957 and 1959. Inversions then are common as are "high" levels of pollution. The danger attends their conjunction and persistence. Relief other than elimination of pollution sources is a function of wind movement to disperse pollution over cities, and secondly, the necessity that in-moving air be cleaner than the air it replaces.

The windrose during inversions can establish the percentage direction of winds which might relieve pollution; the wind speed, combined with wind direction, will indicate these tributary areas over which the wind will pass to relieve pollution. These areas should be substantially free of pollution sources.

The concentration of pollution sources in Philadelphia cover an area fifteen miles by ten miles with the long axis running approximately northeast. Let us assume sulfur dioxide to be the indicator of pollution (830 tons per day produced), an air height of 500 feet as the effective dimension, an air volume to be replaced of approximately 15 cubic miles, a wind speed of four mph, selected as a critical speed. Then one cubic mile of ventilation is provided per mile of windspeed and it is seen to require three and three-quarter hours for wind movement to ventilate the long axis, two and one-half hours to ventilate the cross axis. Thus, the tributary to ensure clean air on the long axis is 15 miles beyond the pollution area, 10 miles beyond for the cross axis. The windrose for Philadelphia during inversions shows that wind movements are preponderantly northwest, west, and

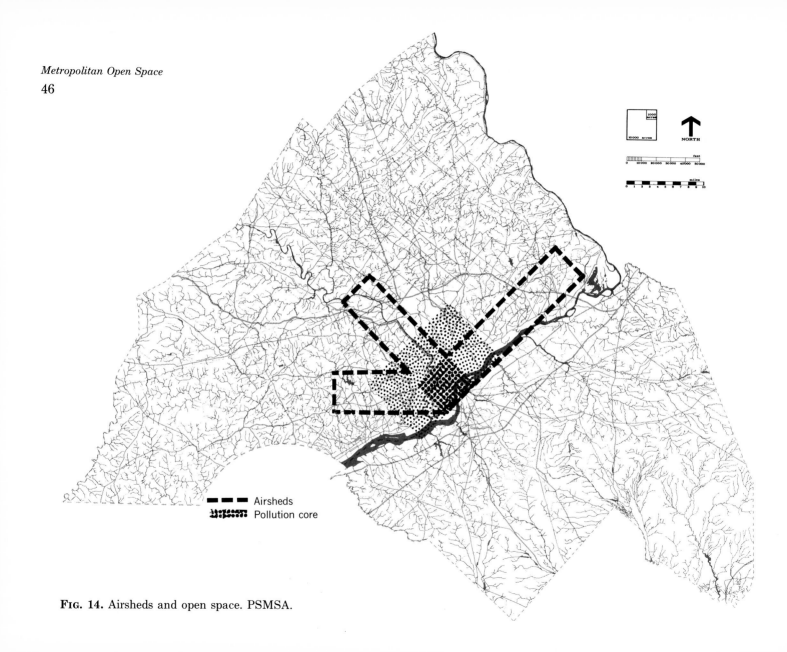

Fig. 14. Airsheds and open space. PSMSA.

southwest, contributing 51.2 per cent of wind movements, the other five cardinal points represent the remainder.

This very approximate examination[17] suggests that airsheds should extend from 10 to 15 miles beyond the urban air pollution sources in those wind directions to be anticipated during inversion. The width of these belts should correspond to the dimension of the pollution core and, in very approximate terms, would probably be from three to five miles. Such areas, described as airsheds, should be prohibited to pollution source industries.

Should this concept be realized, broad belts of land, free of industry, would penetrate radially toward the city center.

Under the heading of atmosphere the subject of climate and micro-climate was raised. In the study area the major problem is summer heat and humidity. Relief of this condition responds to wind movements. Thus, a hinterland with more equable temperatures, particularly a lower summer temperature, is of importance to climate amelioration for the city. As we have seen, areas which are in vegetative cover, notably forests, are distinctly cooler than cities in summer, a margin of 10° F. is not uncommon. Air movements over such areas moving into the city will bring cooler air. Relief from humidity results mainly from air movement. These correspond to the directions important for relief of inversion. We can then say that the areas selected as urban airsheds are likely to be those selected as appropriate for amelioration of the urban microclimate. However, in the case of the former, it is important only that pollution sources be prohibited or limited. In the case of microclimate control, it is essential that the airsheds be substantially in vegetative cover, preferably forested.

17. Study on the Philadelphia airshed conducted under direction of the writer by Hideki Shimizu, Department of Landscape Architecture, University of Pennsylvania, 1963, unpublished.

The satisfaction of these two requirements, in the creation of urban airsheds as responses to atmospheric pollution control and microclimate control, would create fingers of open space penetrating from the rural hinterland, radially into the city. This is perhaps the broadest conception of natural process in metropolitan growth and metropolitan open space distribution. Clearly, this proposal directs growth into the interstices between the airshed corridors and suggests that metropolitan open space exist within them.

CONCLUSIONS

In summary, it is proposed that the form of metropolitan growth and the distribution of metropolitan open space should respond to natural process. The phenomenal world is a process which operates within laws and responds to these laws. Interdependence is characteristic of this process, the seamless web of nature. Man is natural as is the phenomenal world he inhabits, yet with greater power, mobility and fewer genetic restraints; his impact upon this world exceeds that of any creature. The transformations he creates are often deleterious to other biological systems, but in this he is no different from many other creatures. However, these transformations are often needlessly destructive to other organisms and systems, and even more important, by conscious choice and inadvertance, also deleterious to man.

A generalized effect of human intervention is the tendency towards simplification of the ecosystems, which is equated with instability. Thus, the increased violence of climate and microclimate, oscillation between flood and drought, erosion, siltation, are all primary evidence of induced instability.

Human adaptations contain both benefits and costs, but natural processes are generally not attributed values, nor is there a generalized accounting system which reflects total costs and benefits. Natural

processes are unitary whereas human interventions tend to be fragmentary and incremental. The effect of filling the estuarine marshes
or felling the upland forests is not perceived as related to the water
regimen, to flood or drought; nor are both activities seen to be similar
in their effect. The construction of outlying suburbs and siltation of
river channels are not normally understood to be related as cause and
effect; nor is waste disposal into rivers perceived to be connected with
the pollution of distant wells.

Several factors can be observed. Normal growth tends to be incremental and unrelated to natural processes on the site. But, the
aggregate consequences of such development are not calculated nor
are they allocated as costs to the individual incremental developments.
While benefits do accrue to certain developments, which are deleterious to natural processes at large, (for example, clear felling of forests
or conversion of farmland into subdivisions), these benefits are *particular* (related in these examples to that land owner who chooses
to fell trees or sterilize soil), while the results and costs are *general*
in effect. Thus, costs and benefits are likely to be attributed to large
numbers of different and unrelated persons, corporations, and levels
of government. It is unprovable and unlikely that substantial benefits
accrue from disdain of natural process; it is quite certain and provable
that substantial costs do result from this disdain. Finally, in general,
any benefits which do occur—usually economic—tend to accrue to
the private sector, while remedies and long range costs are usually
the responsibility of the public domain.

The purpose of this study is to show that natural process, unitary
in character, must be so considered in the planning process, that
changes to parts of the system affect the entire system, that natural
processes do represent values and that these values should be incorporated into a single accounting system. It is unfortunate that there
is inadequate information on cost benefit ratios of specific interven-

FIG. 15. Rivers, steep slopes, and flood plains—among proper determinants of metropolitan growth.

tions to natural process. However, certain generalized relationships have been shown and presumptions advanced as the basis for judgment. It seems clear that laws pertaining to land use and development need to be elaborated to reflect the public costs and consequences of private action. Present land use regulations neither recognize natural processes, the public good in terms of flood, drought, water quality, agriculture, amenity or recreational potential, nor allocate responsibility to the acts of landowner or developer.

We have seen that land is abundant, even within a metropolitan region confronting accelerated growth. There is, then, at least hypothetically, the opportunity of choice as to the location of development and locations of open space.

The hypothesis, central to this study, is that the distribution of open space must respond to natural process. The conception should hold true for any metropolitan area, irrespective of location. In this particular case study, directed to the Philadelphia metropolitan region, an attempt has been made to select certain fundamental aspects of natural process, which show the greatest relevance to the problem of determining the form of metropolitan growth and open space.

The problem of metropolitan open space lies then, not in absolute area, but in distribution. We seek a concept which can provide an interfusion of open space and population. The low attributed value of open space ensures that it is transformed into urban use within the urban area and at the perimeter. Normal urbanization excludes interfusion and consumes peripheral open space.

Yet as the area of a circle follows the square of the radius, large open space increments can exist within the urban perimeter without major increase to the radius or to the time distance from city center to urban fringe.

The major recommendation of this study is that the aggregate value of land, water, and air resources do justify a land use policy which reflects both the value and operation of natural processes. Further, that the identification of natural processes, the permissiveness and prohibitions which they exhibit, reveals a system of open space which can direct metropolitan growth and offers sites for metropolitan open space.

The characteristics of natural processes have been examined; an attempt has been made to identify their values, intrinsic value, work performed and protection afforded. Large scale functions have been identified with the major divisions of Upland, Coastal Plain, and Piedmont; smaller scale functions of air and water corridors have been identified; and, finally, eight discrete parameters have been selected for examination.

For each of the discrete phenomena and for each successive generalization, approximate permissiveness to other land uses and specific prohibitions have been suggested. While all are permissive to greater or lesser degree, all perform their natural process best in an unspoiled condition. Clearly, if land is abundant and land use planning can reflect natural process, a fabric of substantially natural land will remain either in low intensity use or undeveloped, interfused throughout the metropolitan region. It is from this land that public metropolitan open space may best be selected.

This case study reveals the application of the ecological view to the problem of selecting open space in a metropolitan region. It reflects the assumption that nature performs work for man and that certain natural processes can best perform this work in a natural or mainly natural condition. Clearly, this is a partial problem; one would wish that simultaneously, consideration were also given to those lands which man would select for various purposes, for settlements, recreation, agriculture, and forestry. Such a study would be more complete than the isolation of a single demand. Yet, it is likely that the same proposition would hold although the larger study would better reveal the degree of conflict. For the moment, it is enough to observe that the ecological view does represent a perceptive method and could considerably enhance the present mode of planning which disregards natural processes, all but completely, and which in selecting open space, is motivated more by standards of acres per thousand for organized sweating, than for the place and face of nature in man's world.

2

The Distribution and Value of Open Land in the Philadelphia Area

NOHAD A. TOULAN

The pattern of urbanization and open land in the PSMSA was examined between 1930 and 1960. There were in 1960 over 1.8 million undeveloped acres out of 2.2 million total in the area. A general land abundance is evident. The value of the open land was $1.7 billion, with $1.5 billion at $960/acre in private ownership. The aggregate value of all lands significant to the water regimen outlined in Chapter I was just over $900 million. Land values varied by distance from downtown Philadelphia, but the distribution of values by sectors was found to be most important in eventual costs of an open space plan.

Ian McHarg has said that the best way to minimize man's interference in natural process is to make metropolitan growth and the distribution of metropolitan open space responsive to natural process. Water is utilized as an indicator to define natural resource areas which

53

should be a major basis for metropolitan open space, albeit not the only one.

Using the water regimen, he defined the natural system to include surface water, marshes, flood plains, aquifers, aquifer recharge areas, forests, steep slopes, and prime agricultural land. The first five have a direct relationship to water, while the next two are water related since they are determinants of water in process. The last is not central to the water regimen although of concern to McHarg because of its irreplaceability.[1] The first seven together are called "natural resource lands" in the succeeding text.

This chapter takes the McHarg principles as points of departure and addresses itself to the question of how much natural resource land is involved in a typical eastern metropolitan area, where it is in relation to urbanization, and how valuable it is at present prices. The purpose here is to set the stage for the legal, economic, and design considerations of possible open space programs.

We deal with the PSMSA as a case study. It measures changes in open land[2] from 1930 to 1960 and considers the amount and distribution of natural resource land identified in Chapter I as significant to the water regimen. The present market value of this land is then calculated and general consideration is given to the aggregate present

1. The preliminary analysis conducted in this study indicated about 249,000 acres of prime agricultural soils. Two-thirds of these (164,000 acres) did not overlap any of the other areas. Since these are not directly related to the water regimen, it was decided to eliminate them from the calculations because of their size and cost. The remaining acres are implicitly included in the figures reported for the particular parameters with which they overlap. No attempt, however, has been made to identify such overlaps.

2. Open land was identified as any undeveloped land or land developed at a lower density than one house per two acres. See above, p. 8. While this allows for many inclusions of land that by other definitions would not be considered open, at the scale of the measurement it was felt to be statistically valid. See Nohad A. Toulan, "Public and Private Costs of Open Space Preservation," University of Pennsylvania, 1965, unpublished Ph.D. dissertation.

values of alternate open space systems varying by location to down-town Philadelphia.

URBANIZATION AND OPEN LAND IN THE PSMSA

The period between 1930 and 1960 witnessed changes in the structure of metropolitan areas which are without parallel in history. Although population grew rapidly, the size and nature of the urbanized area increased at a much faster rate. In 1930, the outer radius of the circle of urbanization around Philadelphia was less than eight miles. It had increased to 16 miles by 1960. The area actually developed increased from 110,000 to 430,000 acres. Relative to the total area of the present PSMSA, urban land represented only five per cent in 1930 but had increased to 20 per cent in 1960.

In this same thirty-year period, more than 15 per cent of the open land in the region became urbanized. In a sense, this is not a great loss considering that the PSMSA still has 80 per cent, or about 1.8 million acres, of its total land area still open. If this is related to the 1960 population, it will be noted that in that year, the PSMSA had one acre of open land for every two persons of its population. However, those lands were not evenly spread over the region nor practically accessible to a large part of its population. The loss of open space was much more serious in areas near the center of the region and almost insignificant in peripheral areas.[3]

Within a five-mile radius of Philadelphia's City Hall, more than two-thirds of all open lands existing in 1930 were developed by 1960. On the other hand, the loss of open land in areas beyond 35 miles from the center amounted to less than five per cent (see Table 2 and Figure 16). More significant than the loss of open space, perhaps, is

3. This, of course, suggests that the Standard Metropolitan Statistical Area is not entirely satisfactory as a unit of analysis in judging the magnitude of open space loss. Availability of data, however, requires its use.

TABLE 2. *Distribution of Urban Land by Distance from Philadelphia City Hall, 1930 and 1960*

Distance from City Hall	1930[1]		1960[2]		Per cent Change in Urban Land 1930–1960
	Urban Land (Acres)	Per cent of the Ring Open	Urban Land (Acres)	Per cent of the Ring Open	
Less than 5 miles	24,500	46.3	38,576	14.2	57
5–9	38,800	73.2	97,840	32.1	152
10–11	11,050	87.5	43,840	47.5	296
12–13	8,890	91.3	32,000	66.5	260
14–15	5,420	95.6	33,552	71.7	519
16–17	4,730	96.4	24,640	81.0	421
18–19	4,000	97.3	27,648	80.9	691
20–21	2,280	98.3	23,008	82.9	1,009
22–23	2,011	98.7	21,056	86.0	947
24–25	1,800	98.9	17,888	89.5	994
26–29	2,910	99.0	30,480	89.8	1,047
30–34	2,600	99.2	25,056	92.3	863
35 and over	1,620	99.6	15,232	96.0	840
Total	110,611	95.1	430,816	80.14	289

1. The acreage computed and measured from the Regional Plan of the Philadelphia Tri-State District.
2. Toulan, Nohad A., *Distribution and Market Values of Open Land in the Phila. Standard Metropolitan Area,* Institute for Urban Studies, University of Pennsylvania, 1964.

the unequal distribution of existing open land. In 1960, for example, less than 15 per cent of all land within five miles of downtown Philadelphia was open while beyond 35 miles, more than 95 per cent of the total area was still open.

Equally important is the extent of scatteration generally characteristic of the contemporary pattern of urban development and frequently blamed for the loss or destruction of open space.[4] The term

4. William Whyte, Jr., "Urban Sprawl" in the *Exploding Metropolis* by the Editors of Fortune, Doubleday, 1958.

56

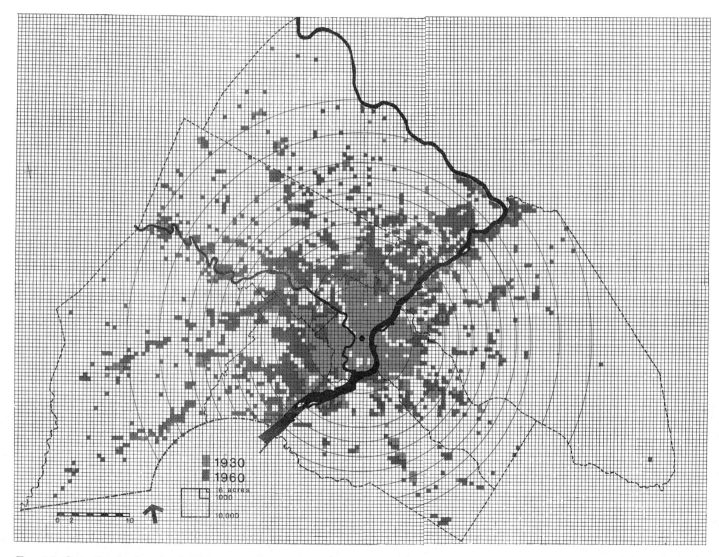

Fig. 16. Growth of urban land 1930–1960. PSMSA.

scatteration can mean scattered communities or it can also mean scattered dwelling units.[5] Land use data were available for the PSMSA in grids, each representing one quarter square mile.[6] Scattered development was defined operationally as isolated developed areas of less than two grids, or 320 acres. On the average, this represents clusters of less than 500 dwelling units surrounded on all directions by open land for a distance of at least one-half mile. Of course a definition of scatteration must give due consideration to the distance between isolated developments and thus what may be termed scattered development in one region is not necessarily so in another depending on the scale and general pattern of development in each.

In the PSMSA, scatteration does not seem to have increased between 1930 and 1960, at least in relative terms. In 1930, isolated developed areas of less than 320 acres (half a square mile) amounted to more than 9,000 acres or about nine per cent of all urban lands. In 1960, the absolute figure had increased almost three times to slightly more than 26,000 acres. Relative to the total acreage of urban land, however, it declined to about six per cent.

Another measure of scatteration is how much open land becomes isolated in small pockets. Applying the same standard used above, it was found that isolated pockets of open land with less than 320 acres amounted to 2,500 acres in 1930, rising to 8,000 acres by 1960 (see Table 3).

5. For a more detailed discussion on the subject of scatteration, see Jack Lessinger, "The Case for Scatteration," *Journal of the American Institute of Planners*, Volume XXVII, Number 3, August 1962, pp. 159–69.

6. Nohad A. Toulan, *Distribution and Market Values of Open Land in the Philadelphia Standard Metropolitan Area*, Institute for Urban Studies, University of Pennsylvania, Phila., Pa.

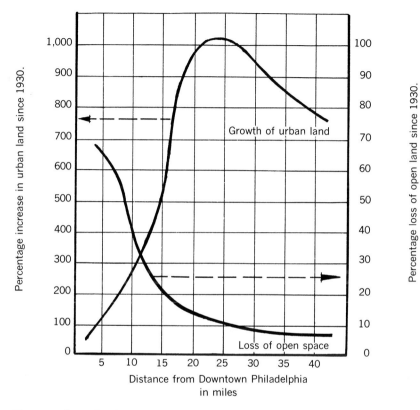

FIG. 17. Growth of urban land and loss of open space, 1930–1960. PSMSA.

SIZE, CHARACTERISTICS, AND OWNERSHIP OF OPEN LAND

In 1960, the PSMSA had 445,984 acres of urbanized land and 1,800,736 undeveloped acres in contiguous plots of 16 acres or more (see Table 4). Of course, not all of this open acreage is in private

TABLE 3. *Scattered Development and Isolated Pockets of Open Land*

	1930		1960	
	Number of grids	Acreage	Number of grids	Acreage
Isolated development less than 160 acres	47	5,600	150	18,000
Isolated development between 160 and 320 acres	16	3,800	35	8,400
Total		9,400		26,400
Isolated pockets of open land less than 160 acres	17	2,000	45	5,400
Isolated pockets of open land between 160 and 320 acres	2	500	11	2,600
Total		2,500		8,000

ownership and to that extent not all of it is equally subject to forces in operation in the metropolitan land market. Public lands, 177,280 acres in all, are least likely to be developed for urban uses. Similarly, semi-public lands, which totaled 34,160 acres, though subject to some pressures from the market, usually offer more resistance to development than land privately owned. The two categories combined represented 12 per cent of all open land in the PSMSA. There was one acre of undeveloped land in public and semi-public ownership for every two urbanized acres.

Most open land was located in large contiguous plots of at least one-quarter square mile. Acreage in smaller areas surrounded completely by urbanization was miniscule in absolute aggregate. Isolated pockets varying in size from 16 to 160 acres accounted for less than 2,500 acres.

Spatial Distribution of Open Land

Reference has already been made to the fact that it is not the lack of open space per se but its distribution which is a major problem. The above figures support the contention that, taking the metropolitan area as a whole, there is an abundance of land. Whether it is well located with respect to the present and future open space needs of the area is, however, another question. In order to establish the basis for an exploration of this matter, the spatial distribution of open land in the area was analyzed. Calculations were made of the amounts

TABLE 4. *Distribution of Open Lands by Distance Rings by Ownership*

Distance in Miles from City Hall, Philadelphia	Total Area	Open Lands		Public		Semi-Public	
		Acreage	% in the Ring	Acreage	% to Open Lands in the Rings	Acreage	% to Open Lands in the Ring
Less than 5	50,400	7,176	14.23	2,592	36.12	240	3.34
5–10	151,200	48,520	32.08	5,216	10.75	960	1.97
10–12	88,960	42,264	47.50	3,840	9.08	1,744	4.12
12–14	101,440	67,440	66.48	3,408	5.05	2,688	3.98
14–16	121,440	87,048	71.67	2,784	3.19	3,056	3.51
16–18* (1)	129,920	105,280	81.03	3,552	3.37	4,000	3.79
18–20 (1)	144,960	117,312	80.92	4,848	4.13	3,936	3.35
20–22 (2)	134,240	111,232	82.86	5,856	5.26	3,040	2.73
22–24 (2)	150,240	129,184	85.98	8,000	6.19	3,536	2.73
24–26 (3)	170,560	152,624	89.48	19,984	13.09	2,384	1.56
26–30 (4)	298,080	267,648	89.79	34,528	12.90	2,384	.89
30–35 (5)	327,040	301,984	92.33	45,344	15.01	4,096	1.35
More than 35 (6)	387,240	363,024	95.97	37,328	10.28	2,096	.57
Total	2,246,720	1,800,736	80.14	177,280	9.84	34,160	1.89

* Beyond 16 miles the parts of the SMSA that fall in the various distance rings are less than the total area of each proportion of each ring in the SMSA are as follows: (1) 95%, (2) 80%, (3) 85%, (4) 63%, (5) 50%, (6) 15%.

of undeveloped acreage on the New Jersey and Pennsylvania sides of the PSMSA, in various sectors on each side, and at various distances from downtown Philadelphia. The results of the last of these sets of calculations proved to be most illuminating and are described briefly in the following paragraphs.

The PSMSA was divided into rings centered on downtown Philadelphia, roughly the center of population. As would be expected, open lands exceed urban lands by a substantial margin in all the outer rings (see Table 4). Within the five mile ring, however, only 14 per cent of the area is open. In the area between five and 14 miles from downtown, the percentage of open land increases sharply to about two-thirds of total acreage. Beyond 14 miles the percentage of open to total land continues to rise, but at a sharply reduced rate since most of the land is open, to about 95 per cent. Of all open land in the PSMSA, less than 10 per cent lies within the 14 mile ring and less than 15 per cent within the 16 mile ring.[7] By contrast, 60 per cent of all such lands are located at distances in excess of 24 miles.

Most public lands are located in the peripheral rings while semi-public lands showed a concentration in the intermediate rings. However, the area with the highest percentage of open land in public and semi-public ownership is the innermost circle. Within that circle of five-miles radius, it was found that 3,000 acres of public and semi-public constitute almost two-fifths of all open lands. By contrast, the more than 49,000 acres of public and semi-public lands in the 30- to 35-mile ring represent only 16 per cent of all open lands in the ring.

Parts of the above analysis can prove slightly misleading since the percentage of open lands in and close to the built up core relative

7. For the Philadelphia reader it may be helpful to note that the sixteen mile radius reaches almost to Paoli, extends beyond Chester nearly to the Delaware state line, includes Norristown, the Willow Grove Naval Air Station, and encompasses Willingboro (Levittown), New Jersey, but not Levittown, Pa.

to total undeveloped acreage is partly a function of the physical size of the PSMSA. For the purpose of this study, we were not concerned with the acreage beyond about a 24-mile radius of Philadelphia's downtown. With a few exceptions, these lands are well outside not only present urban boundaries but future ones as well. If attention is focused, therefore, on land lying within the 24-mile limit (approximately 1,100,000 acres), a somewhat more realistic picture emerges. Undeveloped land totals two-thirds, rather than four-fifths of all acreage, and almost one-fifth of open land is located within the 14-mile boundary. Less than one-tenth of all open land is protected by public or semi-public ownership, and 70 per cent of the original public acreage now falls outside the area completely. Finally, average value of undeveloped acreage is considerably higher, as would be expected.

LAND VALUES AND THE LOCATION OF OPEN LAND

As part of the process of determining costs of open space preservation, estimates of the aggregate value of open land were made and an isovalue map was prepared to show relative values of land in the region.[8] The land in the PSMSA which is still open was found to have an approximate total value in 1962 of $1.7 billion. If public and semi-public lands are eliminated, the aggregate value drops to about $1.5 billion, representing an average of $960 per acre.

Natural resource lands having one or more of the six[9] natural characteristics were slightly cheaper than lands where none of these

8. All land sales reported in the Real Property News published by the Philadelphia Board of Realtors were plotted for the two-year period 1961-62. Rough isovalue lines were drawn. These were checked in the field and corrected by local appraisers.

9. It should be noted that actual measurement included large rivers, subsumed small streams, etc., under the nearest land category, and included only that portion of prime agricultural land also in another category. This reduced the categories from eight to six.

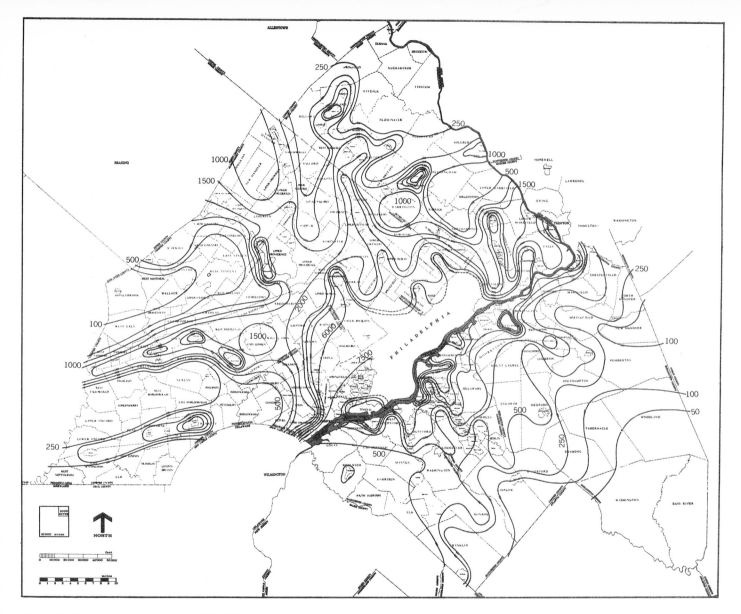

FIG. 18. Isovalues of open land, PSMSA.

parameters exist. The former averaged $950 in value against $980 for the latter. The aggregate value of all lands significant to the water regimen was just over $900 million, or slightly over half the value of all land.

The distribution of value of open lands follows trends similar to those reflected by distance rings. Most of the open acreage was in areas where land was cheap. Slightly more than one million acres, representing 56 per cent of all open lands, were in areas where the average market value per acre was less than $500. The significance of this figure lies in the fact that $500 per acre is the upper value limit which is generally ascribed to farm lands in this region. In contrast, only 52,000 acres, representing four per cent of all open lands, were in areas where the average value per acre was in excess of $5000 (see Table 5). The remaining 40 per cent of the lands ranged in value from $500 to $5000 per acre. They are located in the developing suburban belt. Interestingly, the aggregate value of the 52,000 acres nearest downtown exceeded the aggregate value of the million acres at the fringe of the PSMSA by a substantial margin.

The distribution of public and semi-public lands by value shows a greater than average concentration of public acreage in areas of cheap values and of semi-public acreage in the intermediate value zones. Areas with average values below $500 per acre accounted for 80 per cent of all open public lands, and over one-third of all lands valued under $100 per acre were publicly owned. On the other hand, almost half of all semi-public lands were found in areas where the value ranged between $500 and $2000 per acre. Open land in the innermost zone, in which land values were in excess of $7,500 per acre, was almost 40 per cent public and semi-public.

The major concentrations of public land in areas of cheap land values is attributable to a considerable degree to the Wharton tract in Burlington and Camden counties. That tract is located in a part of the region which is undergoing urbanization at a negligible rate. Most open lands in its vicinity whether privately or publicly owned are still in the wild state of nature and, with the exception of a few areas where timber and cranberry bogs might be harvested, offer little development opportunity. Even so it should be mentioned that the pine barrens, of which the Wharton Tract is a part, receive intermittent consideration as megalopolis' new supersonic jetport. The high percentage of public lands in the inner zones is due to the fact that much of the open land in these areas is in regional and local parks such as the Fairmount Park in Philadelphia and the Cooper River Park system in Camden County.

TABLE 5. *Distribution of Open Lands by Value*

Value in Dollars	Total Area	Open Lands		Public		Semi-Public	
		Acreage	% in the Zone	Acreage	% to Open Lands in Zones	Acreage	% to Open Lands in Zones
More than 7500	93,720	13,760	14.68	4,880	35.46	416	3.02
6000–7500	60,800	17,072	25.55	1,840	10.77	928	5.43
5000–6000	50,360	21,120	41.93	2,288	10.83	1,232	5.83
4000–5000	56,080	26,112	46.56	2,208	8.45	1,520	5.82
3000–4000	83,080	46,960	56.52	2,096	4.46	2,432	5.17
2000–3000	134,440	88,880	66.11	4,464	5.02	3,328	3.74
1500–2000	190,088	142,768	75.10	5,232	3.66	7,216	5.05
1000–1500	176,800	141,632	80.10	2,720	1.91	4,336	3.06
500–1000	327,360	283,120	86.48	6,592	2.32	4,576	1.61
250–500	382,400	352,656	92.22	16,768	4.75	2,880	.81
100–250	399,680	384,912	96.30	26,880	6.98	3,136	.81
50–100	133,120	130,224	97.82	45,888	35.23	2,160	1.65
Less than 50	152,000	151,520	99.68	55,424	36.57	—	—
Total	2,246,720	1,800,736	80.14	177,280	9.84	34,160	1.89

The concentration of semi-public lands in the intermediate zones relates primarily to the nature of the institutions that own these lands. Most of the acreage is owned by golf clubs and other private recreation facilities that require proximity to the urban area. These facilities are likely to yield to developers when the pressure on them becomes great and when their land values rise. This explains their relative absence in the inner zones.

VALUES OF OPEN LAND BY SECTORS

The pattern represented by the lines of equal values,[10] clearly indicates that land values vary substantially from one sector to another within the region and not just with distance from the center. Understandably this is due to the fact that growth trends are different in the various sectors. This fact, however, raises an important point, namely, that although the cost per acre of preserving open land would decline with distance from the center, in some sectors open land can be preserved closer to downtown for the same cost as in a much more distant area within another sector.

In some sectors urban growth has been rapid while in others slow. In the former (active development) land values decline fairly gradually within the zone where development is active, but near the outer edges of this zone they suddenly drop very rapidly. Beyond that drop, the curve levels and the decline of values by distance becomes insignificant (see Figure 19). In sectors of the second type (inactive development) the sharp decline in values starts closer to the center of the region and its drop is usually less gradual than in the first case. The behavior of the two curves in peripheral areas is almost identical (see Figure 20).[11]

10. Toulan, *op. cit.*

11. In all sectors the possibility exists that secondary urban centers may result in a sudden rise in land values. This, however, does not change the shape of the basic curve unless it is of an enormous magnitude.

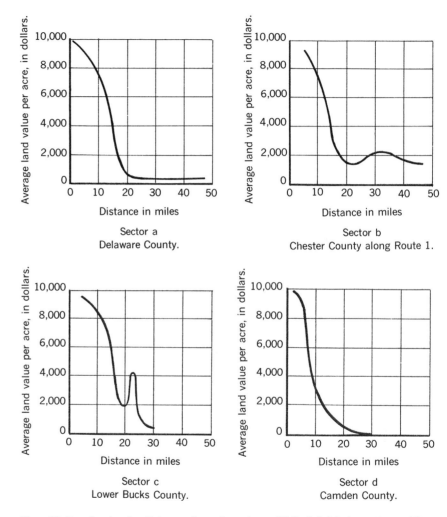

Fig. 19. Land value by distance from downtown Philadelphia in sectors with rapid urban growth.

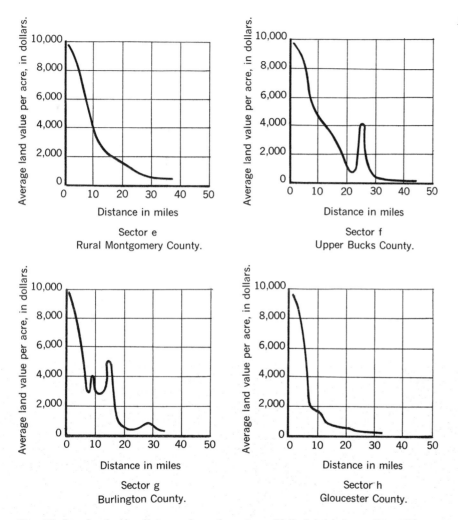

FIG. 20. Land value by distance from downtown Philadelphia in sectors with slow urban growth.

The immediate implication of this is to suggest that the overall cost of preserving open space will not depend solely on its location relative to the core of the region.

NATURAL RESOURCE LAND

Although the emphasis in the later discussion on controls is on less-than-fee acquisition, that is on regulation, it was conceived at one point in the study as possible that public agencies in the PSMSA might acquire most of the areas characterized as significant for the water regimen and meet regional recreational and other open space requirements within these same areas.

In order to give an order of magnitude to the acreage and money requirements for any such program, and to determine what alternate programs of acquisition and controls might be conceived, the study identified all of the land within the categories of aquifers, aquifer recharge areas, forests, marshes, steep slopes, and flood plains. Water, although important, was eliminated because, with few exceptions, it will remain undeveloped and in smaller streams was subsumed under the nearest land category. Prime agricultural land was measured and then only that part (one-third of total) which also fell within another class was included in the following calculations.[12]

Undeveloped land having one or more of the six physiographic characteristics of special value to the water regimen amounted to about 1,128,000 acres, or slightly less than two-thirds of all open lands. About 15 per cent of land in this category was in public and semi-public ownership (see Table 6).

Among the six types of undeveloped land, forests included by far the largest number of acres (almost 600,000; see Table 5). This amounts to one-third of all the open lands in the region, and more

12. See footnote 9.

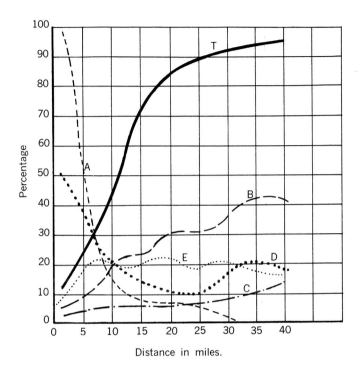

T ▬ Percentage of open land

A _ _ _ Percentage in Acquifer Recharge

B _ _ _ Percentage in Forests

C .__. Percentage in Marshes

D**••••** Percentage in Steep Slopes

E .... Percentage in Flood Plains

FIG. 21. Distribution of ecologically valuable open land by distance from downtown Philadelphia.

TABLE 6. *Summary Distribution of Physiographic Phenomena Philadelphia Standard Metropolitan Statistical Area*

Type of Area (Phenomenon)	Acreage	% to Total Open Lands	% in Public, Semi-Public	Total Value of Privately Owned Lands in $(000)	Value per Acre of Private Lands
Aquifers	149,455	8.29	3.47	218,895	1,520
Aquifer Recharge	83,058	4.61	6.57	240,976	3,100
Forests	588,816	32.69	23.88	262,685	580
Marshes	133,984	7.44	30.60	25,289	275
Steep Slopes	262,064	14.55	8.16	281,103	1,170
Flood Plains	339,760	18.86	19.43	244,790	890
Sub total*	1,127,772	62.62	14.8	914,717	953
Other greenlands	672,964	37.38	5.9	611,510	970
Total greenlands	1,800,736	100.00	11.73	1,526,227	960

* Adjusted for the overlap between the types of areas.

than one-half of the combined acreage of the six parameters. Ranking second were flood plains with a total of about 350,000 acres or slightly less than one fifth of all open lands. At the other end of the scale, aquifer recharge lands encompassed less than 100,000 acres or only five per cent of all open lands. Steep slopes, aquifers and marshes accounted for 15 per cent, 80 per cent, and seven per cent of all open lands respectively. Some land, of course, fell into more than one category. These were forested steep slopes, forested flood plains, marshy flood plains, and so on. Overlaps, however, involved only one-third of the acreage (see Table 7).

In evaluating open space policy alternatives and setting priorities, it is obviously important to know the extent to which various categories of land are already protected from the incursions of urban development. In the PSMSA it is interesting to note that one-third of all marsh land, one-quarter of all forest lands, and one-fifth of all flood plains are already in public and semi-public ownership (see Table 5). The other three types of land occur in areas predominately in private ownership. In general, these acres were also the most expensive and thus presumably the most difficult to preserve whether by acquisition or other means.

The Value of Natural Resource Open Land

In 1962, all privately owned open land in the PSMSA had an aggregate value of one and one-half billion dollars with an average value of $960 per acre. The total value of land privately owned significant to natural process outlined previously amounts to slightly more than $863 million with an average value of about $970 per acre. Less than one per cent of the acreage significant to the natural process is in areas with average land values in excess of $7,500 per acre, but its aggregate value represents more than five per cent of the total. At the other end of the scale, almost 60 per cent of all such land is

TABLE 7. *Summary of the Area Overlaps of Physiographic Phenomena**

Number of Phenomena	Acreage		$ in Public and Semi-Public	Total Value of Privately Owned Lands in $(000)	Value per Acre of Private Lands ($)
	Total	In Private Ownership			
One	749,411	654,385	12.7	579,046	897
Two	263,055	224,753	14.9	268,814	1,196
Three	108,033	74,260	31.5	58,386	786
Four	6,625	6,300	4.9	7,986	1,268
Five	648	648	—	543	838
Total	1,127,772	960,346	14.8	914,717	953

* Aquifers as the most pervasive and least directly vulnerable have been ommitted from these calculations to introduce more practicality in the figures. McHarg cites the aquifer recharge areas, which are included above, as the most vulnerable access points to the aquifers. See Chapter I, p. 37.

TABLE 8. *Distribution and Aggregate Value of Privately Owned Land Significant to Natural Process*

Average Value per acre	Acreage		Aggregate Value in $(000)	
	Amount	Per Cent	Amount	Per Cent
Less than $500	523,749	58.3	107,830	12.5
500–1,999	254,749	28.5	285,200	33.0
2,000–4,999	87,320	9.8	272,470	31.5
5,000–7,500	25,079	2.8	151,000	17.5
More than 7,500	4,712	.6	47,120	5.5
Total	895,509	100.0	863,720	100.00

in areas with average values below $500 per acre and its value amounts to only one-eighth of the total.

Table 8 indicates that if the primary interest is to preserve the largest amount of land possible, almost 60 per cent of all natural resource land could be acquired in fee simple for slightly more than one hundred million dollars. On the other hand, if the concern is primarily with areas close to urbanization nearly two hundred million dollars would be needed to acquire less than 3.4 per cent of the acreage.

Table 9 indicates that in terms of average value per acre, the most expensive of the five elements[13] are aquifer recharge areas, because they are concentrated along the Delaware River in highly urbanized areas. Land in this category had a value of $240 million, or $3,100 per acre. Marsh land on the other hand, also heavily concentrated along the Delaware, is the cheapest, with an average value of $275 per acre and an aggregate value of slightly more than $25 million. Forests, which have the largest acreage, are next to marshes in the average value per acre. Their aggregate value is slightly more than $262 million.

13. See Table 6, p. 72.

In general, the distribution of the five elements in the PSMSA is such that the most expensive ones are those requiring the least restriction on land use, while marsh land, which may have to be acquired in fee simple, is the cheapest of all. In other regions it may be expected that marshes will always be in areas with cheap land values, but aquifer recharge areas will not necessarily follow the same pattern as in the Philadelphia area.

Distribution and Value of Characteristics by Distance from Center of Region

Three of the five categories, forests, marshes, and flood plains, tend to increase in acreage as the distance from downtown Philadelphia increases, while the reverse is true for aquifer recharge areas and steep slopes (see Figure 16).

Aquifer recharge areas are mainly concentrated along the eastern bank of the Delaware River, a part of the region which is highly urbanized. Within a radius of five miles from downtown Philadelphia, 90 per cent of all open land is aquifer recharge. In the second five-mile

TABLE 9. *Value of Land Significant to Preservation of Natural Process (1962 dollars)*

Elements*	Value of Privately Owned Land in $(000)	Value per Acre
Aquifer recharge	$240,796	$3,100
Forests	262,685	580
Marshes	25,289	275
Steep Slopes	281,103	1,170
Flood Plains	244,790	890
Total**	$863,720	965

* See Table 6, p. 72.
** Adjusted to eliminate the overlap between the five elements.

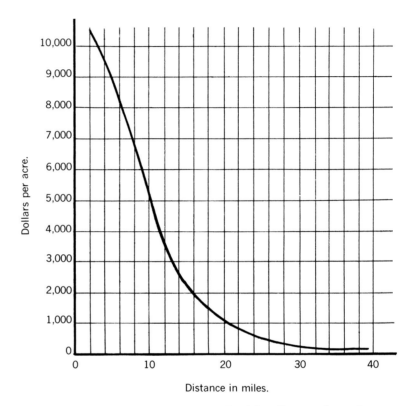

FIG. 22. Average value of undeveloped land by distance from downtown Philadelphia.

ring, however, its relative size drops to about one-quarter. Beyond the ten-mile radius, the size of aquifer recharge areas relative to all open land acreage drops from more than ten per cent in the eleventh and twelfth mile to less than three per cent in areas between 25 and 30 miles, and to complete absence (*beyond* the 30-mile) ring. The distribution of aquifer recharge areas in absolute number of acres, however, does not indicate any major concentration in any distance ring. Out of the 13 distance rings into which the region was divided, aquifer recharge areas occur in eleven in almost equal proportions (see Table 10).

The presence or absence of marshes in an area is to a large extent a function of urbanization as well as drainage. This has been reflected along the Delaware River where the majority of marshes have already been filled in. Due to this, there are virtually no marshes within the

TABLE 10. *The Distribution of Open Land by Distance: The Philadelphia Standard Metropolitan Statistical Area, 1960*

Distance in Miles from Downtown Philadelphia	Open Land Acreage	% to Total Area	Aquifer Acreage	% to Open Land	Aquifer Recharge Areas Acreage	% to Open Land	Forests Acreage	% to Open Land	Marshes Acreage	% to Open Land	Steep Slopes Acreage	% to Open Land	Flood Plains Acreage	% to Open Land
Less than 5	7,176	14.23	13,280	88.28	6,610	92.11	432	6.02	—	—	720	10.03	3,320	46.26
5–9	48,520	32.08	33,344	56.35	12,032	24.79	5,936	12.23	1,152	2.37	10,304	21.23	12,816	26.41
10–11	42,264	47.50	22,016	42.62	4,720	11.16	8,544	20.21	2,112	4.95	7,520	17.79	8,000	18.92
12–13	67,440	66.48	16,992	19.26	4,464	6.61	14,976	22.20	4,128	6.12	11,968	17.74	13,032	19.32
14–15	87,048	71.67	17,200	16.31	8,648	9.93	19,584	22.49	3,808	4.37	12,992	14.92	15,976	18.35
16–17* (1)	105,280	81.03	16,656	13.92	8,544	8.11	25,056	23.79	4,208	3.99	13,840	13.14	22,440	21.31
18–19 (1)	117,312	80.92	13,728	9.99	7,400	6.30	35,248	30.04	7,648	6.51	12,448	10.61	25,144	21.43
20–21 (2)	111,232	82.86	12,304	9.26	7,592	6.82	34,144	30.69	8,736	7.85	10,512	9.45	24,984	22.46
21–23 (2)	129,184	85.98	11,968	7.71	8,248	6.38	36,480	28.23	6,432	4.97	12,432	9.62	23,328	18.05
24–25 (3)	152,624	89.48	11,136	6.64	7,928	5.19	48,544	31.80	8,928	5.84	14,816	9.70	28,608	18.74
26–29 (4)	267,648	89.79	13,328	4.60	6,872	2.56	83,024	31.01	18,768	7.01	33,904	12.66	53,712	20.06
30–35 (5)	301,984	92.33	4,448	1.14	—	—	125,024	41.40	20,544	6.80	57,680	19.10	52,512	17.38
More than 35 (6)	363,024	95.97	—	—	—	—	151,824	41.82	47,520	13.09	62,928	17.33	55,888	15.39
Total	1,800,736	80.14	186,400	8.29	83,058	4.61	588,816	32.69	133,984	7.44	262,064	14.55	339,760	18.86

* Beyond 16 miles the parts of the SMSA that fall in the various distance rings are less than the total area of each.
The percentages of each of these rings that falls in the SMSA are as follows: (1) 95%, (2) 80%, (3) 85%, (4) 63%, (5) 50%, (6) 15%.
Source: Toulan, Nohad A. op. cit. Distribution and Market Values of Open Land in the Philadelphia Standard Metropolitan Area.

first ten miles.[14] Three-quarters of all marshes are in areas beyond 24 miles from downtown Philadelphia, while one-half are beyond 30 miles. In general, the occurrence of marshes in the various distance rings reveals no particular trend other than a tendency to increase gradually as the distance from the core of the region increases.

Almost one-half of the flood plains are located in areas beyond 26 miles from the center. The acreage of flood plains relative to that of open land in the various distance rings reflects a relatively even distribution in the region. The rings with the highest and smallest percentage of flood plains are the first and last rings, respectively. In the first, flood plains constitute almost one-half of all open lands, whereas, in the last ring, they represent only 15 per cent. In between these two rings the ratio of flood plains to open land is fairly constant with minor variations below and above the 20 per cent mark.

Steep slopes are also concentrated in outlying areas. About 60 per cent of them are in areas beyond 26 miles. Less than one per cent are within a five mile radius from the center. The rest of the acreage is distributed almost equally among the nine distance rings between 5 and 25 miles.

Forests are most affected by urban growth and expansion. Marshes may be filled in, flood plains built upon, and steep slopes leveled, but none of these modes of land preparation is easier for the developer than the removal of forests. However, the destruction of woodlands in most cases takes place long in advance of urbanization since farmers must clear land for agricultural use. Forests are not concentrated in one major cluster. Rather, they are fairly well distributed throughout the region with a higher frequency of occurrence in outlying areas. Two-fifths of all forests are in areas beyond 26 miles, while only three per cent are within the first 12 miles. The ratio of forest to open land

14. Much of South Philadelphia was once marshland.

Zones	Area of Private Open Lands Acres	Percent in One or More of the Parameters	Aggregate value of all private open Lands $(000)	Value per Acre $
Heavily built area	40,368	73.8	277,992	6,890
Inner suburban belt	276,224	58.7	680,020	2,460
Outer suburban belt	406,528	53.2	372,184	915
Agricultural belt	866,176	63.7	196,029	225

in the various distance rings reflects to some extent the impact of urbanization. In the first five-mile circle, only six per cent of all open land is in forests. On the other hand, in areas beyond 30 miles, forests represent more than two-fifths of all open land. In between these two points, the percentage of open land in forests increases steadily with the distance from the center.

Relating the general distribution of the five categories to the degree of urbanization indicates that their size relative to the overall size of the open land tends to decline as we move away from the heavily built area around the core (see Table 11). In that zone, mainly because of the dominance of aquifer recharge areas, the five categories combined represent about three-quarters of all open land. This proportion declines to 59 per cent in the inner suburban belt and to slightly more than half in the outer suburban belt. It increases, however, to 64 per cent in the agricultural belt where forests and steep slopes are abundant. Translating this in terms of values it means that, outside of the agricultural belt, the proportion of land requiring preservation or other conservation treatment is higher in areas where average land values are high and declines as the average value declines.

SUMMARY

This chapter summarizes the relative values and distribution characteristics of land significant to natural process in the PSMSA. It is evident that with a given amount of money, a wide range in amounts of land can be controlled or acquired. In the absence of information on the relative importance to the water regimen of various characteristics, along with their significance for development, recreation, or amenity, a priority system for their retention cannot yet be set up. This problem is considered in some detail in Chapter IV.

When that information is available, based on more detailed scientific study, then the degree of intervention which can be tolerated in the water regimen as related to other values can be ascertained and combinations of land control and regulation can be set up as the possible outcome of a least-cost solution, or optimizing method.

In the meantime, it is very evident that the 1962 aggregate land value of all areas ($863 million) significant to the water regimen is so sizeable as to, on the face of it, point up the necessity of considering any possible programs in light of major emphasis on uncompensated regulation and less-than-fee acquisition and control. Chapter III following outlines possible regulations and controls, and sets up a hypothetical model that shows the range of reductions in total cost possible by their application.

3

Incentives and Controls for Open Space

ANN LOUISE STRONG

This article considers what combinations of land use restrictions and land use controls, enacted by what public agencies, are best suited to realization of the goal of protection of natural resource land for the Philadelphia SMSA. Emphasis in the recommendations is on long-term protection of the natural resource system, rather than on low initial cost or greatest immediate public acceptability.

Selection of land use controls is related to the drop in market value caused by the land use restrictions: uncompensated regulation is recommended when the drop is 25 per cent or less; compensated less-than-fee controls for a drop of 26 to 76 per cent; and fee acquisition when the drop is 76 per cent or greater.

A preference is stated that, where a choice exists, regional public agencies should enact the controls affecting natural resources because of the regional nature of the resource system.

The open space identified by the physiographic analysis exists today in the Philadelphia area. It exists, but as of this writing, it is being nibbled away voraciously by developers. At the same time, local and state governments here and across the country anticipate early acquisition of substantial open space through state[1] and federal grants. This and similar studies are particularly timely because of the need for guidance of the public programs as they come in contact and conflict with urban growth.

In any large metropolitan region there is certainly a limit as to how much land can be preserved without hindering or harming urban growth. When this limit is reached is not known. It does appear, however, that acquisition of large tracts by public agencies has not yet occurred on such a scale as to adversely affect housing markets. Previous acquisitions, therefore, are not likely to provide guidelines for future actions and the question still remains as to how much land can be withdrawn from private ownership or restricted from development before it becomes costly and difficult for the market to adjust itself.

In the Philadelphia area, for example, in the period between 1930 and 1960 more than 140,000 acres were acquired or donated to public agencies,[2] and about 59,000 additional acres were placed under various forms of lease agreements for hunting grounds and for the protection of game and fish.[3] Moreover, several tens of thousands of acres are under zoning regulations restricting their development to very low

1. E.g., the "Green Acres" program of the State of New Jersey and "Project 70" of the Commonwealth of Pennsylvania.

2. In 1930 the Philadelphia Tri-State District Plan reported that the acreage of public lands in the eight county metropolitan areas was 37,000 acres. Today there are 177,000 acres of public lands.

3. Ann Louise Strong, *Open Space in the Penjerdel Region*, Table 3, p. 15, Penjerdel, Philadelphia, 1963.

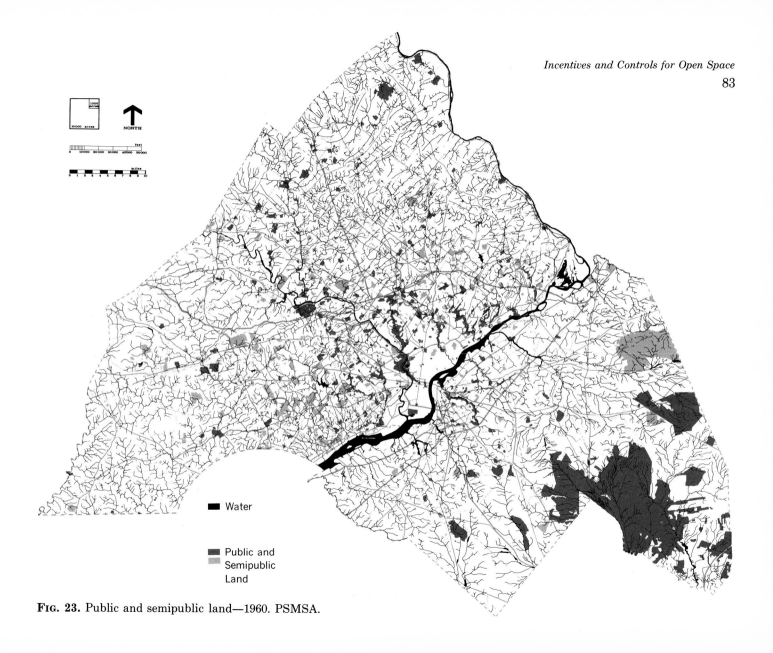

1000 acres

10 000 acres

NORTH

feet
0 10 000 20 000 30 000 40 000 50 000

miles
0 1 2 3 4 5 6 7 8 9 10

■ Water

■ Public and
Semipublic
Land

FIG. 23. Public and semipublic land—1960. PSMSA.

densities. With the exception of areas zoned for low density development, however, the bulk of lands acquired, received through donations, or leased was in peripheral areas where land values are low and where pressures on land to develop are negligible. In addition, more than one-half of all lands brought into public ownership are in the Wharton Tract in Burlington and Camden counties of New Jersey.[4]

Public acquisition of land in the Philadelphia area during the thirty year period between 1930 and 1960 raises two important points. In the first place, public acquisitions and leases amounted to 200,000 acres even though there was no special program or organized action to preserve open land. Secondly, almost all of that acreage was, when acquired, in peripheral areas, and most of it is still in areas with very low development potentials. This means that the experience is of relatively little value in terms of examining the impact of potential acquisition or controls.

THE GENERAL QUESTIONS

The general questions addressed by this chapter are: What means now exist for implementing an open space program based on the general purposes and principles outlined previously? How effective are they? How and where should they be used, alone or in concert, and what will be their impact? What agencies should or can carry out the implementation?

Answers to these questions are inextricably entwined with answers to questions about future demands for land, allocation of these demands, and the economic and fiscal impact of implementation of open space recommendations. Finally, law, as the basis for land use controls and incentives, is the heart of implementation.

The inquiry into controls and incentives is founded on one major premise, namely that the natural resource areas to be protected are

---

4. See Chapter II, p. 65.

part of a functionally logical natural system—that of water in process—and that the water regimen as the major indicator of many related processes is important to man's well-being, perhaps to his survival.

Controls and incentives for parts of the system must be adopted with the objective of protecting the total system, thus helping nature to perform its many tasks, but particularly those of flood control, water storage, and water purification, which are the most easily identified and quantified. Vital by-products of protection of the system will be provision of recreation areas and preservation of natural amenity in the metropolitan area. Also, since the concern for the system is a long-range one, the controls and incentives should be chosen as much on the basis of continuing efficacy as low initial cost or ease of implementation.

In the PSMSA eight physiographic phenomena or types were selected as of dominant importance for the system of water in process. Seven of them, surface water, marshes, flood plains, aquifers, aquifer recharge areas, steep lands, and forests, have been demonstrated to be clearly related to the water regimen. (The eighth, primary agricultural soils, is the least easily justified in terms of its role in the water regimen[5]). Elsewhere, water may also be the dominant factor in natural resource protection, and yet the dominant land types and the controls necessary to sustain their hydrologic function may differ from those selected here. However, the approach to implementation of the system should have general applicability.

A few general observations are in order before discussing specific incentives and controls for the seven directly water-related types.[6] First, preserving the hydrologic function of the land does not neces-

5. See Chapter II, p. 54.
6. Note that although Chapter II reduced the significant measurement to five types, the sixth and seventh, aquifers and surface water, are included in this discussion because of the legal problems involved.

sarily assure that the land will continue in open space use. Therefore, realization of recreation or amenity goals may require imposition of additional controls, along with additional justification based on other than the water argument. Second, the selection of controls must be made with reference to judgments concerning the character, location and volume of the current and future demand for land for development. Third, the seven types discussed frequently overlap, occurring in approximately forty combinations. To preserve the hydrologic functions of each combination, controls for each of the coincident types must be applied in conjunction with one another.

The discussion of incentives and controls stresses public, affirmative action. Public agencies bear primary responsibility for implementation of public plans, and emphasis on their role should minimize neither the importance nor the efficacy of private organizations. Affirmative controls receive most consideration because, while negative controls also are influential, it is far more difficult to affect the time and location of action through their use.

THE IMPLEMENTING AGENCIES

Water in process, and the physiographic phenomena related to it have been termed part of the "seamless web" of nature.[7] In contrast the public agencies empowered to preserve these functions form a many-seamed and multi-layered web. Unless there is a clear allocation of responsibility for preservation of resource functions, this latter web will have gaps as well as overlaps. Naturally, local governments should act where misuse of resource areas within their boundaries threatens the health and safety of their own occupants. Where resource areas extend beyond local government boundaries or where the threat arising from misuse of one resource area is to persons or property

7. See Chapter I, p. 21.

elsewhere, action by an agency empowered to act on a regional basis is probably necessary, although action through intergovernmental cooperation is a possibility.

In the Philadelphia SMSA, the municipalities and counties can act only locally, while the Delaware River Basin Commission, a major new governmental device created by a federal-interstate compact, can act on a regional basis.[8] Because the Delaware River Basin Commission's mandate covers water resource management and because it is both charged with development of a plan for use of the water resources of the basin and empowered to implement much of such a plan, the Commission is the logical government agency to carry out many of the recommendations of this study. At the same time, all other units of government should introduce a major concern for natural process into their land use planning. In other areas of the country, this latter may be the only immediate hope, short of state intervention, that is possible.

OPEN SPACE INCENTIVES

Discussion of the role of public agencies in implementing open space plans tends to obscure the political reality that such programs must be supported by the general public. Support can come only as a result of a widespread agreement on open space as a necessary and desirable goal, and it is a major objective of this study to help stimulate consensus in this direction.

To date, incentives for open space have been mainly private—the concern of the conservationist, of the nature lover, and of the sportsman. Individuals have banded together to save the Tinicum Marsh

8. Authorized by a federal-state compact in 1961 between the Federal Government and the states of New York, New Jersey, Delaware and the Commonwealth of Pennsylvania, the Commission got underway in June of 1967. Its mandate is planning and management of water resources.

Wildlife Refuge, part of the Brandywine Valley, the Big Sur, and other areas of great natural beauty and unique function.

Nevertheless, until these private incentives or motivations are translated into public incentives, they will remain fragmentary and consequential in only a limited sense. Therefore, it is appropriate to focus concern on public incentives, of which there are currently few, but a powerful few.

In charting a course for protection of the natural resource system, legal shoals must be avoided. Some are obvious and well marked; others, largely because of the application of old devices to new situations, remain unexplored and hazardous. Space here permits but a cursory scanning of a few.

Public incentives for open space preservation take three forms, all financial in nature. Money may be given or tax relief granted by one level of government to induce other levels of government or private landowners to hold land open. Regulations may permit higher densities—and higher profits—in return for preservation of open space.

In the Philadelphia SMSA, incentive programs now operative provide grants from the federal government to state and local governments, from the states to local governments, and from a county to its municipalities. All of the grants provide for acquisition of land or interests in land for open space purposes.

Tax laws, both federal and state—the second financial incentive—are primarily for private, but to a lesser extent for public, preservation of open space. Tax relief includes exemptions, charitable deductions, and preferential assessment.

The third form of public open space incentive is experimental. A number of zoning ordinances permit a higher overall intensity of use if open space also is provided. New York City gives additional floor area ratio potential where setbacks exceed minimums. This kind of formula can also be applied in suburban areas. Cluster zoning may not permit higher densities but may be more profitable because of lower infrastructure and development costs. These incentives have certain limitations inherent in zoning itself in that the open space-density ratios must be based on some systematic standard to be defensible and must not depend on unrealistic changes in housing preferences.

LEGAL SETTING FOR CONTROLS

While these incentives can be significant in achieving open space, direct legislative controls are more likely to provide open space in substantial amounts. Choice of land use controls and the public agency to exercise them is determined largely by a decision as to the most effective means of implementing open space plans at lowest cost. However, the restraining arm of the law also influences this choice. The decision makers must have a sense of legal limitation on each type of control, as well as knowledge of the scope of enabling legislation for public agencies, in order to select controls. Because preservation of urban open space for other than public parks is quite a new public undertaking, many of the governing legal principles must be deduced by analogy to other fields in which they have been operative previously. Often public agencies have not exercised the open space powers granted them by enabling legislation. This means that there has been no litigation and, consequently, no delineation of legal limits of these powers. However, enough is known or deducible to state some guiding principles for the general legal issues which arise in conjunction with urban action to preserve open space.

Several challenging areas of legal inquiry related to means of controlling use of open space have been selected for brief examination here. Considered are: the power to regulate, its extent and exercise; the breaking points between regulation, less-than-fee controls, and fee acquisition; and preferential tax treatment.

REGULATION AS DISTINGUISHED FROM ZONING AND SUBDIVISION CONTROLS

Within the open space framework, zoning and subdivision controls are regulation, but not all regulation is zoning or subdivision control. Since the distinction between the terms leads to differences in their applicability, it is important to define them carefully at the outset and to state that they will be used as defined throughout this chapter.

Regulation is defined as uncompensated control of activities for the public health, safety, morals, and welfare; in this context it is control of land use for open space purposes. Zoning and subdivision controls are defined as one form of regulation, included within the overall definition but with two qualifications: (1) they encompass the entire geographic area of the enacting unit of government, and (2) the public for whose benefit they are enacted are the residents of that unit of government, not people at large. Regulation of the flood plain of a stream throughout its course, enacted for the benefit of people at large, irrespective of their place of residence, would not be termed zoning under this definition.

The distinction made here is of importance in order to clarify the limitations in the grant of zoning and subdivision control powers to local governments. For instance, it would be improper for a local government, acting under zoning powers, to prohibit cutting and development of forest land on the ground that increased runoff would add to flood damages of an entire watershed. Similarly, the local government would lack authority to prohibit development of an aquifer recharge area for the purpose of maximizing the quantity of flow to an aquifer serving a nearby metropolitan area. These regulatory powers might be specifically delegated by a state, possibly to local governments, but more probably and more logically to a regional public agency charged with resource management.

State Regulatory Power Is Possible

The states have broad powers to regulate man's use of his resources. Power to regulate through use of zoning and subdivision controls customarily has been granted by the states to local governments and has been widely used by them, in part for resource objectives. The retained power of the state to use zoning and subdivision controls often has been neglected. In fact, to date, only Hawaii has chosen to exercise the state zoning power. Other regulatory powers granted by the states to local governments are restricted to protection of persons within the boundaries of the local government. It remains for the states to employ their general regulatory power to control use of resource areas for the benefit of the public at large, not just the public in the areas regulated.

Dedicated Open Space Must Be Directly of Benefit to Users

As an illustration of what has just been said, to be sustained as reasonable, subdivision requirements for the dedication of land for open space or payment of a money equivalent should be tied, for acreage standards, to population density in each subdivision and, for facility standards, to total population in the subdivision. The open space, if not within the subdivision, must be easily accessible to the residents. If too far away, regulations requiring it may be challenged successfully by the developers.

No Taking Without Just Compensation

The above, or any kind of land use regulation, will be held unconstitutional as a taking without just compensation, if it causes too great a drop in the market value of land when applied. Already it is accepted that landowners, through regulation, may be deprived of some portion of their land's value; the need is to quantify and stand-

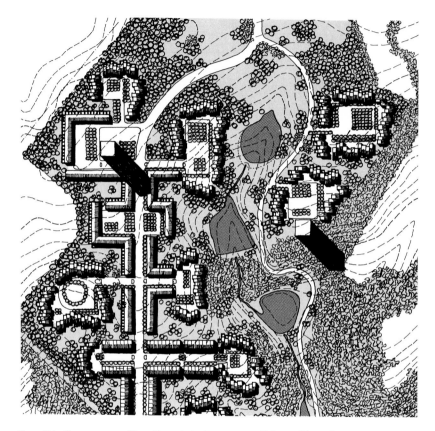

Fig. 24. Open space directly related to users. (Mays Chapel Village, Md.)

ardize the permissible per cent of loss. To date, there has been no presumption of unconstitutionality based on a given per cent of loss attributable to regulation. Here it is later proposed, for open land, that all losses in excess of 25 per cent attributable to regulation be presumed unconstitutional. Therefore, uncompensated regulation would be used only for land use restrictions causing a drop in market value of 25 per cent or less.[9]

While regulations deprive landowners of varying percentages of land value, landowners receiving compensation for land use controls are paid the full value of their loss. For example, zoning might reduce a parcel's value 15 per cent, while the owner of a similar parcel, reduced in value 15 per cent by a utility line, would be paid the full value of that right-of-way. This is an inconsistency in present public policy that quite possibly should be eliminated so that all landowners subjected to land use controls would bear the same proportionate cost of these public controls. Such an approach is defensible for owners whose land is subject to public less-than-fee interests, but it is arguable that, because of the inconvenience and dispossession accompanying fee acquisition, full loss compensation should continue to accompany fee acquisition.

Validity of Controls over Time

Controls customarily are chosen for their cheapness and efficacy at the time of selection. Regulations, valid when enacted, could become unreasonable because of lack of compensation, and thus invalid, as a result of rising land values. Should an estimate of future rise in value be one factor used in selecting land use controls? Alternatively, should future increase in value be rejected, by law, as a ground for invalidation of controls?

Planning Controls to Establish Assessed Values

Preferential assessment of open space violates the *ad valorem* tax principles included in most state constitutions. If preferential assess-

---

9. See *Infra,* p. 122.

ment of open space is authorized by law or constitutional amendment, this action weakens the real property tax structure and encourages subsequent breaches in it. Lower taxes on open space can be achieved instead by use of planning controls which restrict land to open space uses and thus cause assessment to be based on land value for these uses only.

A State Capital Gains Tax

A state capital gains tax could be imposed on all land sales in which there had been an increase in intensity of residential use since the last prior sale. Revenues from this tax would be allocated to support of open space land use controls. A capital gains tax of this character would pose a uniformity problem under state constitutions but might be sustained as a reasonable classification for purposes of taxation.

Controls for Open Space

Present powers for open space control are, if properly applied, sufficient for preserving far more open space than has resulted so far. Public concern and support is necessary to increase and enlarge their use. The following discussion of controls for open space is divided into the three major purposes considered earlier: (1) the concern for natural process concentrating on balancing the water regimen; (2) provision of areas, largely coincident with those necessary for (1), but for recreation purposes; and (3) amenity. It is, of course, the hypothesis of the study that these three purposes can all be served best by following the methods outlined in the study.

CONTROLS FOR NATURAL PROCESS

Each of the physiographic phenomena distinguished previously is here considered in terms of the nature of the controls required to keep it in a natural or near natural state, and to limit development to varying degrees. Then the most appropriate agencies for such control are suggested.

Controls for Surface Water

Surface water and its adjacent, or riparian lands and banks should be subject to controls in order to reduce flooding, to regulate the supply, and to maintain flow and quality. Natural flow patterns are frequently altered through construction of dams, reservoirs, and channel works.

Pollution of surface water can be controlled by regulation so as to sustain adequate water quality for domestic and industrial consumption, for healthy fish and shellfish, and for recreation. However, for pollution regulations to be adequate in a densely settled area such as the PSMSA, they should be based on basin-wide plans for pollution control. Here, the Delaware River Basin Commission can be expected to develop the plan and to share with other levels of government in its enforcement.

Several units of government, from the Commission to municipalities, plan to construct dams and reservoirs which will minimize flooding and husband the area's water supply. If recreation use of surface water is contemplated, rights of access and shoreline acquisition will be necessary. In some instances, scenic easements protecting the view of water from highways may provide sufficient recreation benefits. Control of riparian lands comes, to some extent, under flood plain control, but not entirely. Where it can be demonstrated that the character of adjacent vegetation and banks are important to the water regimen, shoreline control will also be necessary. It is often this adjacent land that provides the greatest amenity and potential for recreation as well as control of water quality.

Fig. 25. Marshes, not drained or filled, retaining their natural function.

Marsh Controls

To fill the resource functions of water storage, water absorption, water purification, and provision of habitat for fish and wildlife, marshes must not be drained or filled. The choice of controls to preserve marshes in their natural state will depend on the extent to which these functions are to be preserved and on the market value of the marshes for other uses.

If public action to preserve marshes will not markedly reduce their market value, uncompensated regulation can be used. If compensation is called for, it can be in the form of compensatory regulations, leases, covenants, or easements. Each has its special role. Fee acquisition would be called for only when heavy public recreation use is desired or when restriction of uses would severely reduce market value.

In the Philadelphia area, most of the marshes are adjacent to the Delaware River. Many have high potential market value for port uses. Where marsh functions are to be preserved, fee acquisition often will be necessary. Here, planning for marsh use should be carried out principally by the Delaware River Basin Commission. Plan implementation is principally a function of the states and local governments.

Aquifer and Aquifer Recharge Controls

The quality and quantity of the water needed for withdrawal from an aquifer will affect the uses which can be permitted in the area which recharges the aquifer. The aquifer itself need be controlled only as to permitted withdrawal, or penetration by canals, injection wells, etc.

To protect water quality in the aquifer, both salinization and pollution must be controlled, the former by maintaining sufficient fresh water flow through the aquifer from the recharge areas and the latter by limiting unsewered land use in recharge areas. Farms, forests, and recreation areas, as well as fully sewered urban development, will be appropriate uses in many recharge areas and over most aquifers. In some, however, where there is a direct connection from surface to aquifer, even sewered development should be restricted because of the inevitable tendency of sewers to leak.

On the other hand, some unsewered uses may be acceptable, depending on the character of the strata and the distance between the recharge area and the aquifer. Controls to protect water quality in the aquifer can take the form of regulation of land use in the recharge areas, with the regulation enacted under the public power to protect health. Whether the regulations should embody performance standards or, instead, fix a range of permissible uses related to various land conditions will depend on detailed knowledge of the relationship between the recharge areas and the aquifers to be protected.

The justification for controlling use of recharge areas to augment the *quantity* of the flow to and from aquifers rests principally on the power to promote the general welfare. Regulation relying on this power probably will fail as an uncompensated taking far sooner than regulation enacted under the public health power. In other words, it is suggested that a greater loss in value of private land can be imposed by regulation when the regulation is enacted for the public health than when it is enacted for the public welfare. To achieve minimum runoff and maximum percolation of water to aquifers, the use of the recharge areas may have to be restricted severely. Limitation of use to open space activities or to sewered development with a 15 per cent site coverage has been recommended in this study as a means of maintaining the quantity of flow.[10] Where land values are low, the necessary use restrictions can be enacted through regulation. Elsewhere in urban areas landowners must be compensated; this can be accomplished by imposing the use restrictions either through compensatory regulations or easements.

The Delaware River Basin Commission already is exercising its powers for planning aquifer use and for controlling recharge areas. Existing state agencies have a supplementary planning role and enact controls for smaller recharge areas.

10. See Table 14, p. 121.

FIG. 26. Flood Plains—not to be built on.

Flood Plain Controls

Preservation of flood plains in their natural state, providing flood waters a place to spread out, lose their momentum, and be stored, is one way of reducing flood damage and of retaining some of the flood flow to recharge aquifers. Uses compatible with fulfillment of the flood plain's water resource functions are those which do not impede flooding, which do not constrict stream flow at flood peaks, and which in turn are not injured seriously by flooding.

Virtually all uses which leave the flood plain land open would be appropriate, including development lots so long as structures and on-site sewage disposal systems were located outside of the flood plain. Of course, for any given flood frequency the contribution of the flood plain to reduced flood damages, the probable costs of flood damages, and the value to the community of permitting various forms of development in the flood plain must be weighed. In many areas, if land use is limited to those uses compatible with preservation of the flood plain's water regimen functions, the restrictions may have a severe impact on market value of urban land.

Because the combination of uses permitted, flood dangers posed, and existing market value will vary from flood plain to flood plain, the land use controls will also vary from regulation to fee acquisition. Regulation might be used where flood plain development would pose a threat to the health or safety of flood plain occupants or to the community at large; it might also be used where land values are low. Compensatory regulations, easements, restrictive covenants, and leases can be used where compensation of landowners is necessary but no public use of the land is contemplated. Fee acquisition may be necessary where land values are very high or where extensive public use of the flood plain is planned.

For the Philadelphia SMSA, the Delaware River Basin Commission should exercise jurisdiction over flood plains whose use affects the basin at large and the water regimen. Local governments should regulate flood plain use where the restraints are needed solely to protect the health and safety of flood plain users in the same jurisdiction.

Forests and Woodlands

Tree cover is maintained to slow water runoff. Trees also have an important effect on microclimate. Some development can be permitted within forested areas without seriously impairing their ability to slow runoff, so long as the site coverage of the development and tree cutting are restricted. Ten per cent site coverage has been suggested as a maximum including structures, roads, and parking areas.[11] Limitation on coverage should be accompanied by restrictions on clearance and cutting of tree cover. For all practical purposes this translates into a density of about one unit to the acre.

Land use controls to preserve tree cover should be enacted as part of the implementation of a river basin plan for regulation of runoff and recharge of aquifers. Regulation may prove adequate for forested uplands far from development pressure. Forested flood plains and marshes often are located in high value areas; where this is so, their preservation will require compensation, through use of compensatory regulations, covenants, easements, leases, and, sometimes, fee acquisition. Where development is permitted in conjunction with tree preservation, the controls would govern site coverage, tree cutting, and alteration of natural contours by grading and filling. If public recreation use of forested land is intended, easements or rights-of-way may be acquired or, of course, the land may be purchased in fee.

In the Philadelphia SMSA, the Commonwealth of Pennsylvania could control use of forested uplands, all of which are located in Pennsylvania, while public agencies at all levels could share responsibility for the forested flood plains and marshes located in both states, and the counties and municipalities could regulate site improvements accompanying development through subdivision regulations.

Steep Slopes

Steep slopes are subject to erosion unless water runoff is checked. Tree cover, or agriculture which incorporates terracing, strip cropping, contour cultivation, and controlled grazing are ways of maintaining

11. See Table 14, p. 121.

FIG. 27. Steep slopes and agricultural land.

such slopes. Rapid runoff from steep slopes also contributes to flood hazards.

Slopes in excess of 25 per cent may best be kept undeveloped, and forested with adequate tree cover to check erosion and runoff. Uses should be limited to recreation and controlled timber cutting. Slopes between 15 and 25 per cent are of course very developable, but site coverage should be limited to ten per cent. This restricts it to either low density development, or high density with low coverage. Such slopes are also usable for agriculture, subject to land management restrictions.

If use restrictions for steep slopes are enacted, not only for water resource management but also to protect would-be occupants from health and safety hazards, then zoning or other regulatory measures can be used. Where the controls are employed to protect the community at large from flood hazards and soil runoff, the type of control may range from regulation to fee acquisition, depending on changes in the market value of the land prior and subsequent to imposition of the land use restrictions. On the slopes in excess of 25 per cent it may be necessary to plant trees in order to assure an adequate tree cover. Owners may voluntarily agree to a public forestation program for their land, but, if they do not, the public must acquire either the fee, and follow up by planting and resale or lease, or an easement for access and planting.

Choice of levels of government control use of steep slopes will depend on the size and regional importance of the areas to be controlled. Hopefully, a river basin plan would determine the importance of maintaining natural cover on steep slopes and would fix standards and specifications for their use. Every level of government from the municipal to the state or regional agency might have a role in implementing this plan.

Prime Agricultural Land Controls[12]

Prime agricultural lands adjacent to urban areas are becoming a relatively scarce resource. Their value for agriculture has declined in the face of agricultural surpluses, and their value as urban building sites has increased, in many instances dramatically. They are perhaps the most vulnerable of the eight classes of land types, but in the present concept of natural process, are less directly significant to the water regimen than the other seven.

Where prime agricultural land does not coincide with and depend for protection on any of the other phenomena, its retention must largely depend on a general consensus as to its amenity value or upon value for agriculture.[13] Where such a case can be made, compensation to owners is very likely required. Conservation districts might be formed to take action for the special purpose of acquiring the fee and selling or leasing back the farmland for farm purposes. State and local governments might act in this way, if appropriate enabling legislation were passed.

For purposes of setting limits on development, examination of existing urban fringes suggests 25 acres as the minimum tract size which will ensure the open quality of the farmland.[14]

Summary

The open space concept advanced in this study uses the water regimen as the principal indicator of the system of natural processes, a system whose health and balance require that certain lands be

12. Included here primarily because of their one-third overlap with other characteristics. They were excluded from consideration as natural resource lands except in Chapter I.

13. For an example of this proposal, see *Plan for the Valleys, op. cit.* It is based on U.S. Department of Agriculture recommendations in the Maryland area.

14. *Ibid.*

retained in a natural or near natural condition. The study identifies the type of lands within the system but has lacked the resources of time and money to determine the specific acreage, location, or combination of these lands that should be held open to sustain the system, to minimize flood damage and to preserve the quality and quantity of the surface and ground water supply. An assumption of this concept is that by-products of preservation of land for water resource purposes will be a significant supply of regional recreation land, and the provision of major elements of natural amenity interfused with urbanization.

Assuming that some portion of each of the types selected might be preserved for its water resource function, it is necessary to consider the incentives available for each type, the controls which might be imposed, the limitations of these controls, and the levels of government which might employ them. Table 12 summarizes who might use what controls to preserve water resource areas.

Where a choice of controls and public bodies is indicated, it is imperative to refer to the text discussion and the more detailed technical reports which resulted from the research to know which combination may be appropriate under any given set of circumstances. Controls best in one location may be unsatisfactory or even unlawful in another location. In addition, a particular level of government may be authorized to employ only some of the possible controls.

Since the water regimen as a part of a system provides the rationale for the study's recommendations, in the Philadelphia SMSA, the controls used to implement the recommendations should accord with the comprehensive water resources plan of the Delaware River Basin Commission. The Commission has been assigned responsibility for planning for use of the water resources of the Delaware River Basin, of which this SMSA forms a part. Its mandate is very broad and can include control of adjacent lands that affect water.

TABLE 12. *Natural Resource Controls**

Resource	Public Body	Possible Controls	Open Space Preserved

Surface Water
1. Pollution Control
   a. land waste
     discharges
   b. boats
2. Water Supply and
   Reservoirs
3. Stream Works
	D.R.B.C., states,
	counties, municipalities
	
	D.R.B.C., states,
	counties
		Regulation	Not
			Necessarily
			
			No

Marshes	D.R.B.C., states, counties, municipalities	Regulation, compensable regulations, lease, covenant, right of way, easement, fee acquisition	Yes

Aquifer and Aquifer Recharge
1. Recharge Area:
   Water Quality
2. Recharge Area:
   Quantity of Flow
	D.R.B.C., states,
	counties, municipalities
	D.R.B.C., states
		Regulation
		
		Regulation, compensable regulations, easements
			No
			
			Yes

Flood Plains	D.R.B.C., counties, municipalities	Regulation, compensatory regulations, easement, lease, fee acquisition	Yes

Forests and Woodlands
1. Forested Uplands
2. Forested Flood Plains
   and Marshes
 	
3. Trees and
   Development
	State of Pennsylvania
	D.R.B.C., states,
	counties, municipalities
	
	Counties, municipalities
		Regulation
		Regulation, compensable regulations, lease, covenant, right of way, easement, fee acquisition
		Regulation
			
			No

Steep Slopes	D.R.B.C., states, counties, municipalities	Regulation, compensable regulations, easement, lease, fee acquisition	Yes
Prime Agricultural	States, counties, municipalities	Regulation, compensable regulations, easement, lease, fee acquisition	Yes

* Exclusive of those which might be imposed by the Federal Government.

CONTROLS FOR RECREATION[15]

The legal justification for recreation space is, of course, based on public use. Consensus regarding standards of amount, quality, and distance affects how much will be needed. Here, the primary concern is with controls necessary to ensure such public use. Of course, a large part of the growing recreation need is for fishing and hunting areas which do not require public ownership. These sports can be accommodated on private land.

The recreation portion of this study, however, was concerned solely with determination of needs for regional,[16] public recreation land. Private areas and neighborhood public recreation land were excluded. Therefore, the discussion of controls of land use will be limited to those appropriate for the preservation of regional, public recreation land to distinguish between the recreation as compared with the natural resource arguments. Land within the regional recreation category is land on which the public must enter to enjoy recreation benefits. Land whose recreation potential is principally visual will be considered under controls for amenity.

Active Public Recreation

Generally speaking, active public recreation areas meeting regional needs should be held in fee by a public body exercising regional responsibilities. However, there are exceptions both to the form of

15. The study of regional recreation requirements for the PSMSA was originally conceived as necessary to helping support the case for open space retention. While Dr. Tomazinis' work developed a method, his results are not central to the natural resource rationale, and therefore his report is being published separately. See p. vi. Nevertheless the legal aspects are considered here because of their interrelation to the legal problems of open space retention.

16. Regional recreation is defined as outdoor recreation for public use, characterized by a time-distance of from one-half hour to two hours one way. It includes fishing, nature walks, swimming and all-day picnics within a single day's trip.

control and to the nature of the public body. It is the exceptions which will be mentioned, since familiarity with them may encourage more variety in approaches to the preservation of public recreation areas.

Leases, rights-of-way, easements and other less-than-fee rights in land may be adequate to assure public use of recreation lands. So, too, may public fee ownership followed by lease or by sale with a right of reverter.

Lands suitable for public hunting may also be used profitably by a private owner, remaining on the tax rolls. The public needs only the right to go on the land during the hunting season. In the Pennsylvania portion of the Philadelphia SMSA, the Pennsylvania Game Commission has leased over 64,000 acres of private land for public hunting. The cost of these leases for acquisition and maintenance combined is about 25 cents per acre per year. Game lands similarly located in the outlying portions of the metropolitan area cost $10 per acre when acquired in fee. Much of this land is hilly and wooded, has no current value for development, and is not economic to farm.

Acquisition of a right-of-way, either temporary or permanent depending on plans for future land use, can provide public access to land for hiking or riding. California's state and county system of bridle trails is evidence of what can be accomplished for public recreation through use of the right-of-way. However, California's difficulties in establishing the trails without the power of eminent domain point up the importance of enabling public bodies to use eminent domain for trail networks.

The Horse-Shoe Trail has its beginning in the Philadelphia metropolitan areas, running from Valley Forge Park 120 miles west to link up with the Appalachian Trail. The Trail has been established mainly by voluntary grants of access by landowners. However, at its eastern urbanized end two municipalities have required developers to dedicate a right-of-way for the trail through their subdivisions.

Affirmative easements can be acquired to provide continuing public access to land as for fishing, picnics, swimming, boating, or skating. The cost of the easement will depend upon the degree to which it restricts other uses and upon the development value of land at the time of easement acquisition.

A public body may acquire the fee to an area, then lease or sell it, subject to restrictions assuring continued public use for recreation purposes. A private golf course might be purchased, then leased subject to the requirement that it be used only for a public golf course. This has already been done by several municipalities in this metropolitan area who have found, to their delight, that this form of purchase and lease is profitable. A mountain slope might be purchased and then leased to a concessionaire for development as a public ski area. Sale subject to a reverter might prove more troublesome than a lease, since legal action would be necessary to enforce the reverter provisions. With a lease, the public body could choose to wait out the lease term and then seek another lessee if the current one performed his duties unsatisfactorily, or it could bring an action to terminate the lease.

Acquisition also can occur under an installment contract although, depending on the terms of the contract, this might postpone public use of the tract until acquisition was complete.

Ideally, regional public recreation land should be acquired by a body charged with this responsibility. In the Philadelphia SMSA the only public body with regional jurisdiction assigned responsibility for regional recreation areas related to water is the Delaware River Basin Commission. However, the counties and the states may acquire land suited in size and location to regional public recreation. In Philadelphia, Fairmount Park is a regional park, and the proposed Schuylkill and Delaware River parks will fill a similar role. Other counties in the metropolitan area, with the aid of HUD's Title VII program,

New Jersey's Green Acres Act, and Pennsylvania's Project 70, anticipate or have undertaken acquisition of regional recreation land. The reservoir site acquisitions proposed by Pennsylvania to implement a portion of the Commission's Comprehensive Plan for water resource management will provide large areas for public recreation.

Recreation Uses of Natural Resource Areas

The major point has been made that areas significant to the balance of the water regimen are also suitable, with various controls, for recreation. For example, surface water is in great and increasing demand for recreation. Recent studies of recreation desires show that the largest unmet demand is for water sports. Recognizing this, an urban area should protect the lakes, streams, reservoirs, and ponds it has and give consideration to creation of new bodies of water by damming. Reservoir construction and stream damming to create farm ponds can have many recreation benefits as well as flood control and water supply benefits. Restriction of construction of stream works may be justified because of the diminution of recreation opportunities which would result.

If the supply of surface water in an urban area is protected and increased, further action may yet be needed to secure sufficient public access to the water. Most riparian land, be it adjacent to a lake or a stream, has considerable value for private residential and recreational development.

The size of water access areas and the public controls used to acquire them for public use will vary with the recreation purpose. Access to water for fishing can be secured by an easement, unless construction of a public livery is also contemplated. Access for boat launching implies presence of a road, ramps, and, if the boats are large, cranes. Parking lots for boat trailers may also be desired. For these purposes, the necessary shore frontage is narrow, but the volume of use and the required improvements make fee acquisition necessary. Where a shoreline beach or park is to be established, fee acquisition is also necessary. If the public recreation consists solely of scenic driving along the shoreline, either compensatory regulations or scenic easements can be used to preserve the view.

Marsh recreation is primarily fishing, hunting, bird-watching, and nature study. All of these activities are relatively solitary, and none alters the natural character of the land, or imposes many requirements for improvements. A trail may be needed or an observation platform but little else. Even though used for recreation, the land can continue unimpeded to fulfill its function as a sponge and a fish and wildlife habitat.

Leases, easements, and rights of way can be used to obtain public access to marsh land for recreation. Usually fee acquisition should not be necessary. Private conservation groups may also acquire land or interests in land to provide wildlife havens as well as nature study areas. In the study area, the Philadelphia conservationists have acquired nature preserves in their own name and have also negotiated the transfer of Gulf Oil Company marsh land to the city for a publicly maintained wildlife preserve.[17]

Obviously, aquifers themselves are without recreation significance. The recharge areas, however, may be ideal for recreation, particularly that which is water-oriented. Since many aquifer recharge areas are located in or adjoining surface water, they are likely to be suited to boating, swimming, and fishing.

Flood plains are almost always suitable for recreation use. The most sharply rising recreation demand is for land with access to water; in the study area, much of this demand can be met by use of flood plain land. The flood plains, possibly more than any other of the land

17. The Tinicum Marsh Wildlife Preserve.

FIG. 28. Tinicum Marsh, Philadelphia.

types selected for protection, are distributed throughout the urban area, providing potential water-related sites for neighborhood as well as regional recreation.

If flood plains overlap with marshes, they can be used for fishing, hunting, wildlife conservation, and nature study. If the land is dry except at flood times, it may be appropriate for picnic areas, beaches, access to marinas, access to fishing streams, and golf—in fact, for a multitude of recreational activities both water-oriented and non-water-oriented. Flood plains held in open space uses can also provide a beautiful setting for scenic roads.

For most recreation on flood plain land, fee acquisition will be necessary. Where private enterprise is willing to act, as in establishing a yacht club, marina, game preserve, wildlife conservation area, or golf course, it can be encouraged. Assuming that the land is already subject to controls which will hold it in uses compatible with its function as a flood plain, existence of a market for private recreation uses may reduce the cost of public controls. If limited public rights are desired, as the right of access for fishing or hunting, easements may be acquired in addition to whatever public controls are in effect to secure flood plain preservation.

In general, forests lend themselves to hunting, hiking, riding, picnics, and scenic driving. Where streams and lakes occur, water sports can also be enjoyed. With clearance of trails, forested steep slopes can be used for skiing. Forested marshes and flood plains may be held as wildlife sanctuaries. The availability of forest land for recreation will, of course, depend upon ownership. When in public ownership, any recreation compatible with forest maintenance will be possible. If the land is private, easements or rights-of-way can be acquired to permit access for hunting and fishing or for a riding and hiking trail. Negative easements can be acquired to protect scenic roads.

For instance, in Oregon, property owners along a portion of State Highway 41 have agreed to preserve a grove of myrtle trees and have given the state an access easement to prune the trees. If a forest area is unique, as for a stand of virgin timber or its botanic specimens, a private conservation organization may be found which can purchase the area, sustain it, and welcome a limited public for education and enjoyment. Only forests sustained in conjunction with development preclude recreation use for any other than the residents of the development. Otherwise, forests and recreation are compatible land uses.

Steep slopes, forested or open, offer limited possibilities for recreation. Skiing comes to mind first, but trails and drives along the slope, offering a scenic outlook, are another potential use. The summit of a hill might also be an attractive spot for a picnic area. None of these recreation activities requires extensive public ownership. For ski areas, control may be obtained by purchasing a base area for parking and service buildings and a sufficiently wide slope area to permit construction of trails. The land can then be leased for operation by a concessionaire or operated by a public recreation agency. Alternatively, a private operator can be encouraged to purchase and develop the area. Scenic trails and drives can be established through right-of-way acquisitions, and picnic areas may be located along their route by purchase of small additional areas. Any level of government operating in an urban region might act to acquire and maintain these recreation areas.

Agricultural land, prime or not, has relatively little recreation potential as such, although it has great visual amenity for urbanites on Sunday drives.

CONTROLS FOR AMENITY

Wherever possible, the legal justification for water resource preservation (or for recreation) should be also used to protect areas of great beauty. But often these are either not enough alone, or are not congruent in their application. Consonant with former President and Mrs. Johnson's concern for natural beauty, and the Supreme Court's decision that cities have a right to use their powers for beauty,[18] the case for controls for beauty alone must be strengthened.

The public need not set foot on the land to derive recreation benefits from it. The Outdoor Recreation Resources Review Commission reported that driving for pleasure is a favored recreational pastime. People also enjoy cycling, riding, or walking along country roads. It is the scenery, as well as the character of the road, which makes these activities pleasurable. The scenery can be preserved for public enjoyment through several forms of public action.

First, outdoor advertising can be controlled by state regulation. Thanks to the pro-billboard lobbyists, this is not an easy task. However, a plan for a network of scenic roads and highways for the urban area should be prepared, accompanied by recommendations for standards and controls. Then legislation should be enacted, designating a scenic highway system and establishing the outdoor advertising controls to be enforced. The proscriptions might be grounded on the state's power to act for the general welfare or for the public safety. For the Philadelphia SMSA, the plan might be prepared by the New Jersey Department of Conservation and Economic Development and by the Pennsylvania State Planning Board. The plan presumably would include all classes of highways from parkways to back country roads, with scenic vistas being the common criterion for their inclusion. In some instances, where there is a narrow visual corridor, only a limited area on each side of the highway need be controlled. Elsewhere, where a view of rolling hills and valleys is to be protected, the outdoor advertising controls must be more extensive.

Not only outdoor advertising requires control to preserve scenic areas for public enjoyment. Other forms of land use also should be

18. See *Berman* vs. *Parker,* 348 U.S. 26, 75 Sup. Ct. 98,99 L, Ed. 27 (1954).

restricted. The nature of the control will depend upon the character of the scenic road and upon the area through which it passes. In this area, the Mill Creek Valley Road in Montgomery County and the Wissahickon Drive in Philadelphia, and in the New York urban area, the Taconic, Saw Mill River, and Hutchinson River parkways exemplify the sense of relative sylvan calm which can be preserved or created in the midst of dense development. Planting, topography, and the presence of streams all contribute to the illusion of space and provide the refreshment of natural beauty. Where urban pressures are great, as in these areas, fee acquisition is practically mandatory to enable a public body to resist development demands. However, as illustrated by the mournful example of Philadelphia's unlovely Schuylkill Expressway, even location of a highway in a public park along a lovely river will not of itself assure pleasurable recreation driving. The highway design must be fitted to the topography, engineered for safety, and landscaped to screen development. Carefully designed, a highway can remain scenic as it penetrates to the heart of an urban area along a narrow corridor.

In more rural areas, where the roads pass areas of limited development, strips could be acquired in fee for the planting of shrubbery as a screen. In presently rural areas or areas of country homes, strips could be acquired to limit use of roadside land. Depending upon land values and topography, these strips might be purchased in fee or easement.

If preservation of an extensive scenic area such as a valley floor is contemplated, the problem becomes more complex and, quite possibly, more expensive. Compatible uses will be low density ones which are harmonious with the natural setting such as farms, institutions, parks, forests, lakes, and reservoirs.[19] If public sentiment places suffi-

19. See *Plan for the Valleys, op. cit.,* for an example.

cent importance on preservation of scenic areas for public visual enjoyment to pay for it, then compensable regulations should be imposed. If, at a future time, it is decided that the cost of the compensable regulations has risen beyond the value of a scenic area to the community, the compensable regulations can be rescinded and development permitted or the public can acquire the land for sale for development. In the absence of a regional public body authorized to preserve scenic areas, the states would be the proper level for action. The states might act through local governments, where scenic areas to be protected adjoin local roads.

Throughout a consideration of means of preserving recreation areas for both active and visual enjoyment, the major premise of this study should be kept in mind, that many needs of an urban area for regional recreation space and amenity can be met from land recommended for preservation because of its natural resource characteristics. Taking the example of the scenic valley, it often includes a stream prone to flooding, with a steep slope bordering the valley on one side and a road marked as part of the scenic highway network on the other side. It should not be forgotten that the public purpose argument sustaining public intervention can be strengthened when the intervention preserves both recreation and natural resource functions.

In the Philadelphia SMSA, a township and private landowners have entered a restrictive covenant to assure preservation of the natural character of a stream valley for the purpose of protecting a scenic drive. The Mill Creek cited before cuts through a steep, wooded valley about five miles from central Philadelphia. A narrow road winds along the stream, crossing it frequently. The covenant, which has been in effect since 1941, restricts use of a strip, from 300 to 500 feet wide, which includes the creek and the road. No buildings, walls or fences may be erected, and trees may be cut only with municipal approval. Dams may be built and existing structures remodeled. The township,

FIG. 29. Mill Creek, Philadelphia.

as its contribution to the bargain, agrees not to widen the two lane road or to permit active public recreation use of the land. Despite high density development in the vicinity, the Mill Creek Valley remains as open and unspoiled as when the covenant was adopted.

Examples like this of areas of unique visual personality exist all across the country. The need is for many more.

Function	Public Body	Possible Controls	Open Space Preserved Through Controls
A. Active Public Recreation	D.R.B.C., States, Counties	Fee acquisition; lease, right of way, easement or other less than fee acquisition; fee acquisition followed by lease or sale subject to restrictions; installment purchase.	Yes
B. Scenic Areas for amenity	States, Counties	Regulation of outdoor advertising; fee acquisition; easement acquisition; regulation; compensable regulation	Yes

THE NEED FOR A PROGRAM AUGMENTING EXISTING CONTROLS

From the previous discussion, it can be seen that a wide range of controls and incentives already are available for most areas. What is desperately needed is an organizing and conceptualizing device to put them to work in concert toward a unified goal, a humane environment.

An open space action program must be based on comprehensive plans which take into account the three purposes—natural resource preservation, recreation, and amenity—emphasized in this study, along with all the other goals which must be incorporated in such plans. Controls now available can go far toward implementing them. In addition, new controls must be tested, and where effective, put into operation. Only by using the various controls and incentives listed as parts of a total program will each be fully effective.

This kind of total program can start with controls now available and, over time, expect that new legislation will permit their progressively accumulating into a more complete and adequate set to implement a planning process.

A METHOD OF COMPUTING THE COST OF THE PROPOSED CONTROLS

For this study, given the controls now authorized in the PSMSA, the next step here is to develop a method of estimating the cost of preserving the water resource functions of any selected portion or all of the natural resource land mapped by Ian McHarg by less-than-fee acquisition. Limitation of use of these lands consistent with resource preservation will require imposition of use restrictions, as discussed above. These restrictions affect market value; this effect, in turn, indicates the type of land use control which may be enacted to impose the use restrictions. Given the effect of the use restrictions on market value, the aggregate cost of the controls can be computed on an estimated basis for any combination of lands included in the system.

The method of computation can be illustrated on a hypothetical basis. First there is a listing of the land categories and possible permissible uses, uses which, hopefully, are consistent with sound water resource management. These uses would vary with location and economic determinants within a metropolitan area. For ease of illustration, only one group of uses is proposed for each land type. Surface water is omitted since it may be controlled by regulation; aquifers are omitted because their protection is dependent on control of the recharge areas.

Next, market value per acre must be determined for these land types, restricted to the uses listed above. To do this, prevailing market

TABLE 14. *Resource Lands: Permissible Uses**

Land Type[1]	Permissible Uses
Marshes	Hunting, fishing, wildlife sanctuary, fish hatchery, utility lines, transmission towers, forestry with selective cutting.
Aquifer Recharge	All marsh uses; farm, park, recreation; sewered development with land coverage limited to 15 per cent.[2]
Flood Plains (50 year)	All marsh uses; farm, park, recreation; development lots so long as structures and sewage disposal systems are outside flood plain.
Forests	All marsh uses; riding and hiking; development with coverage limited to 10 per cent.
Steep Slopes (25 per cent)	Tree preservation required; forest; farming; hunting, hiking, riding and skiing.
(15–25 per cent)	All of above; development with coverage limited to 10 per cent.

1. Where land types overlap, the most restrictive use category will apply.
2. Coverage includes roads, parking areas, driveways, and structures.
* See also Chapter I, p. 43.

value of the land types, unrestricted by the proposed resource controls, must be known. Both the unrestricted values and the restricted values will vary depending on the location of the land, including its proximity to present urbanization, highways, and utilities, as Toulan has indicated.

Assume, for illustration, three value classes with ranges from $0 to $500, $500 to $2000, and $2000 to $8000 per acre, with midpoints of $250, $1250, and $5000 per acre. The market value per acre for the resource lands restricted, would then be estimated for each of the three value classes, using as a guide the value class midpoints, corrected for the particular land type or combination of land types.

Once the per acre estimates of drop in market value, attributable to the land use restrictions, are known, the form of control can be selected. For the purposes of the metropolitan area cost estimate, controls will be limited to three types—regulation, compensated nonfee, and fee. Since active public use is not essential for preservation of the resource characteristics of any of the land types, each of the three types of controls is potentially of equal applicability, and the choice between them will be made solely on the basis of impact of use restrictions on market value.

Regulation will be assumed when the restrictions reduce market value by 25 per cent or less, compensated nonfee controls when the drop is over 25 per cent and no more than 75 per cent, and fee acquisi-

TABLE 15. *Land Use Controls: Cost Estimation Method*

Example of Land Type	Permitted Uses	Value Class Midpoints/ Acre Based on Distance from Core	Value/Acre Corrected for Land Type	Market Value/ Acre, Restricted	% Reduction	Acres Restricted	Control	Cost
Marshes and flood plains	Hunting, fishing, wildlife sanctuary, fish hatchery, utility lines, transmission towers, forestry with selective cutting.	a. $ 250	$ 225	$200	11%	2,000	Regulation	None
		b. $1,250	$1,125	$563	50%	3,000	Compensated non-fee	3,000 × $1,125 × .50 = $1,687,500
		c. $5,000	$4,500	$900	89%	5,000	Fee	5,000 × $4,500 = $22,500,000

tion when the drop is over 75 per cent. If regulation is to be used, there will be no cost for the controls. If compensated nonfee controls are used, the cost will be total acres multiplied by the per cent which the restricted market value is of the value class midpoint, corrected for the land type. If fee acquisition is indicated, the cost will be the total acres multiplied by the value class midpoint, corrected for the land type.

Use of this approach will assist a metropolitan area in choosing land use controls and in arriving at an approximate cost for any chosen combination of areas to be preserved. Areas can be selected for resource importance, location, cost, or any mix of these factors to which a metropolitan area gives greatest weight. In accord with the reasoning set forth in this chapter, no weight has been given to the effect of time on land values. Also, there is no consideration of the result on remaining open land values of large-scale preservation of open space. Therefore, the cost figures obtained from this formula are those for a fixed point in time and in application of the method must be adjusted accordingly.

While it would be more satisfying, and more satisfactory, to offer a formula reflecting the impact of changing conditions, this must be left to the future. There is enough legal and economic uncertainty to make such an attempt most treacherous at this time. Certainly, the choice of land use controls as presently exercised carries with it an intuitive judgment about future land values. To arrive at a reliable appraisal of which type of control will be most effective over time at lowest cost, however, requires a collection and analysis of data beyond the scope of this study. Hopefully, the approach proposed, if implemented, will provide some further knowledge in the spheres of law and economics and will contribute to later work on the problem. Consideration of some of the economic questions raised is in the following chapter by Dr. Grigsby.

4

Economic and Fiscal Aspects of Open Space Preservation

WILLIAM G. GRIGSBY

Resistance to programs for the preservation of large amounts of undeveloped land in metropolitan areas is based in part on the argument that economic costs would be greater than benefits. Advocates of preservation are challenged to prove the contrary. The analysis here suggests that within wide limits economic costs are actually unimportant, so unimportant, in fact, that detailed consideration of benefits at this level of analysis is unnecessary. The probable cost of open space programs to the public sector is, however, quite large, so the question of benefits cannot be permanently avoided. Unfortunately, too, quantitative data which relate the contribution of specific types of undeveloped land to specific open space goals are lacking. As a consequence, fairly arbitrary choices must be made. One set of guidelines which may partially resolve this dilemma is presented.

Historically, arguments, for preserving large expanses of natural open space within urbanized areas have been primarily an aesthetic reaction to a visually displeasing man-made environment and the loss of amenity associated with urban development. The major thesis of the study of which this chapter is a part enlarges the frame of reference to include the question of the adverse impact of badly situated development on certain natural processes that affect water supplies and flood control. Based on fragmentary data, however, the roots of the argument for open space preservation are still very subjective. As a consequence, a need has been expressed for more research and, in particular, detailed cost-benefit analyses, in order to determine how much and what kinds of urban open space are in fact desirable. Given the widespread concern over the disappearance and desecration of beautiful landscape, the question can be asked as to whether economic considerations are appropriate to the discussion. When government will, without too much debate, spend as much as ten million dollars a mile for highway development, is it fair to ask the conservationist to itemize costs and benefits of an open space program which, for an entire metropolitan area, may cost less than a few miles of expressway?

Probably not. Yet to those charged with public decisions, economic questions are important. Although it would be unfortunate if government officials relied more heavily on the abstractions of the dismal science than on the realities of their dismal surroundings, economic analysis can contribute to an understanding of the problem. It can give dimension to some of the issues and distinguish some of those which are irrelevant. The principal purpose here, therefore, is to help illuminate general economic and fiscal questions relating to urban open space planning and to discuss general policy guidelines as they relate to the Philadelphia SMSA.

GENERAL QUESTIONS

Basically, the concern over open space is that neither the private market mechanism working within the present framework of public constraints nor the public sector itself seems to provide the types, quantities, and qualities of space in the locations that layman and expert alike feel it should. Specifically, current preservation efforts proceed on the implicit or explicit assumptions that: (a) there is a deficiency of public and possibly an excess of private open space;[1] (b) a deficiency of near-in and an excess of far-out open space; (c) a deficiency of open space associated with certain natural features of land, water, and subsurface characteristics which act to preserve water supplies and reduce the danger of floods; (d) a deficiency of space in large bundles or linear patterns that give a "feel" of openness. It has never been presumed, however, that there is a deficiency of open space per se. Given a population and an area of a given size, the only way in which *total* open space can be increased is by reducing site coverage, principally through less single and more multi-story construction. For metropolitan areas as a whole, excess coverage is not the problem, though, as will be shown, the proportion of construction in multi-storied structures can possibly be affected by decisions regarding open space preservation.

Fundamentally, then, the issues concern the *positioning* of open space, and obversely, the positioning of development.[2] The major policy questions concerning the distribution of open space within urban areas are how much space, for what purposes, where, for whom,

1. In this context, private open space includes ordinary private yards but not private golf courses and other undeveloped areas which are open to a portion of the public. For the empirical parts of the study, however, open space was defined to exclude most yards. See p. 54.

2. For a similar point of view, see Stanley B. Tankel, "The Importance of Open Space in the Urban Pattern," in *Cities and Space,* Lowden Wingo, Jr., ed. (Baltimore: Johns Hopkins University Press, 1963), p. 59.

in what size parcels, and how reserved. When these questions are approached head on, enormous conceptual and measurement difficulties arise.

For example, if natural open space reserved for public benefit is viewed as an economic good which satisfies certain wants, then like other economic goods, it has substitutes. Thus large-lot zoning provides residents in such areas with certain open space amenities and recreational opportunities that would have to be provided publicly in developments on quarter-acre lots or in rowhouse neighborhoods. Equally, where the purpose of open space is visual amenity or privacy, protective landscaping can in some cases serve as a substitute for more acreage. Further, since there is always open space at the edge of an urbanized area, better transportation to the edge is a partial substitute for more open space closer to center.[3] Numerous other examples of substitutability could be cited, but the degree to which various kinds of open space can be satisfactorily replaced by other kinds of space or by nonspace substitutes is in most cases immeasurable.

The matter of open space for whom is just as perplexing. Objection has frequently been raised to running superhighways through scenic areas. Yet in lessening the amenity value of these areas for the few who care a great deal about completely unmarred natural beauty, highways have brought the amenities of open space to the many. In such situations, it is extremely difficult, if not impossible, to measure the gains and losses.

Rather than grapple with these measurement problems and with equally difficult issues having to do with the preservation of natural processes which protect us from floods and depletion of water supplies, it may be possible to avoid them by raising two separate questions. First, what are the economic costs, just the costs and not the benefits,

3. Except that improvements in transportation permit greater dispersion of activities and thus an extension of the edge.

of preserving more open space in urbanized areas? Second, what are the money costs to government (hereinafter called "public costs")? If the major economic costs can be shown to be either very large or very small, some of the questions listed above become of academic interest only. The same is true for public costs. If they are huge, they may defeat preservation efforts. If they are small, even the most ardent nature lover may be able to have enough trees and green grass. In other words, depending on the magnitudes involved, it may be possible to deal analytically almost exclusively with the cost side of the ledger. This tactic is pursued in the following section.

ECONOMIC COSTS OF OPEN-SPACE PRESERVATION APPEAR INSIGNIFICANT OR UNIMPORTANT

The open space problem arises when open space "uses" and urban uses come into competition for the same land and the former lose out, as is usually the case. If government intervenes to preserve undeveloped land that would otherwise be urbanized, there are nearly always economic costs involved. This is true even if the land is already publicly owned. It is the purpose of this section to discuss these and other costs and their implications for public policy.

The most obvious consequence of protection of any material amount of open land from the encroachment of urban uses is a rise in market values and rents both within the already urbanized area itself and in the still undeveloped areas at the fringe. Thus, in Figure 30, where A is an urbanized area, B the undeveloped fringe, and C an outer unurbanized ring, if B is preserved as open land, urban growth has either to jump to C or take place more densely in A. Assuming growth would occur in both places, market values and rents in both places would of course rise. If growth took place only in C, market values and rents in A might still rise because of its larger differential locational advantage over C than over B. If growth took place only

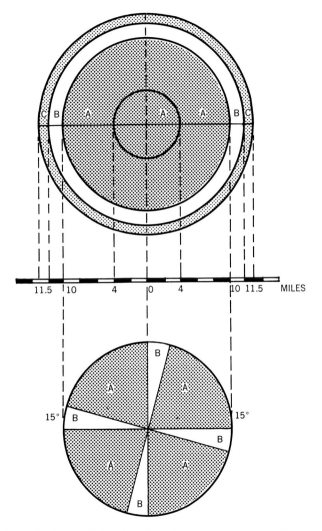

Fig. 30. Hypothetical metropolitan open space patterns.

in A, as might happen if A contained bypassed land, market values and rents in C might remain unchanged.

The same results would be expected even if open-space preservation took a radial form, as in the B areas in Figure 30. The important point to realize, however, is that these changes in the structure of market values and rents are not economic costs, but are merely an imperfect reflection of such costs. Society as a whole incurs no cost if rents go up in A or C.[4] There is only a shift in payments from one group to another. The real economic costs of open space preservation relate to the greater time-distances and residential densities that may result from such a policy. These are examined below.

Time-Distance costs

If developments were shunted from B to C and the urbanized area thereby scattered, journeys to work and other trips might become longer for parts of the population, and this would be a real cost even if these trips also became more pleasurable in the process. Of course, to the extent that B served a recreational purpose, some trips for residents in A would become shorter. In fact, if the ratio of population in A to population in C were high enough and the recreational use of B great enough, perhaps the total cost of moving persons and goods would be less if B were left open than if it were developed. As the work week becomes shorter, this is not an unreal possibility.

The cost of open space preservation in B to residents of C depends on how much interaction there is between A and C and with what parts of A the interaction takes place. Thus, if the residents of C who work in A are employed in the outskirts of A, they would probably regard the extra time of crossing B less costly than if they worked

---

4. Although municipalities, if more than one is involved, may suffer or benefit differentially.

at the center of A. That is, the marginal burden to the worker of an extension of work-journey from, say, thirty to forty minutes is probably greater than an extension from ten to twenty minutes.[5]

There are two additional costs of dispersal that open space preservation may create. One is the extension of sewer laterals and other utilities over "dead" areas, and the second is the displacement of urbanization from its "normal" path onto land that might be more expensive to develop. It should be emphasized, however, that these additional costs are not necessary consequences of preserving open land. Much depends on the topography and the pattern and density of development.

Density Costs

Turning to the higher densities that may result from open space preservation and the cost attached to these changes in density, there are two analytically different situations. The first involves the loss of private open space within the urbanized area, and the second is concerned with the greater unit costs of high-rise construction that higher densities may cause. Suppose that every family in A (Figure 30) has a two acre plot, and that one-half of these families are displaced for a park. If they are forced to move to two acre plots in B, time-distance costs increase as explained above. Similarly, however, if they are accommodated by reducing the sizes of the plots of the families who were not displaced, this might be regarded as an amenity loss against which the amenity of the park must be measured. The amenity loss would vary from family to family depending on personal preferences and might not be very great in the example cited.

5. Although this may vary depending on what the worker expects, which in turn may vary with the size of the urban area. Thus, in Annapolis, Md., the trip may be considered long if over 5 minutes; in Baltimore, long if over 15 minutes; in Philadelphia, long if over one half hour; and in New York, long only if over one hour.

But if the urbanized area were already fairly dense, say four or five families to the acre, and open space acquisition forced a shift to either row housing and apartments, or to longer work-journeys, the marginal amenity loss might be much greater. In the case of high-rise construction, real and measurable economic costs would be incurred as well. Furthermore, materially higher densities in the developed areas might stimulate more trips to the open areas than would otherwise occur. These, clearly, would be an additional economic cost, but must be balanced against shorter work-journeys of a more compactly settled population.

If there is a single idea that emerges from the above discussion up to this point, it is simply that the marginal economic costs of open space preservation inside urbanized areas probably increase with the amount of land preserved, and that if attempts were made to preserve "excessive" amounts, there would be compensating reactions within the rest of the metropolitan system that might be costly and perhaps undesirable.[6] This is hardly a startling observation. The important question is whether there is any way to judge what is "excessive" without extensive calculations based on empirical data.

Some feeling for whether the amounts of land that open space proponents might like to preserve are great enough to pose serious conflicts with other urban land use requirements can be obtained from the geometry of the situation. For example, assuming in Figure 30 a radius for A of ten miles, if the entire core of A were cleared to a radius of four miles, thus opening up one-sixth of the developed area, this would push urbanization outward by only an additional 0.8 mile. Similarly, if B with a width of 0.8 mile were preserved in open uses, this would force urbanization to occur in C for a distance of only 0.7 mile, assuming no increase in density in A.

6. One reaction, desirable or otherwise, might be the decentralization of some employment.

A similar result would, of course, be obtained regardless of the shape or location of the open space. Thus, in Figure 30, if four areas of fifteen degrees each (the four B sections) were converted into park land, thereby opening one-sixth of the previously developed area, urbanization would be pushed outward less than one mile. In addition, in this situation no resident would be farther than approximately four miles from the urban edge. The aggregate cost of hundreds of thousands of slightly longer trips, if longer trips did in fact result from this pattern, might be significant, but it is doubtful that many would consider this cost important.

It is also unlikely that the extra cost, if any, of serving a more dispersed area with public utilities would be significant either in the examples just cited or in most situations.[7] Finally, since the reservation of open space would disperse the urbanized area very little, it is doubtful whether this policy would cause significantly higher densities in the already developed areas. Even if as many as one-half of families "displaced" by the open space policies described in the examples above did move into already developed areas instead of relocating at the fringe, average residential density in these areas would be increased by only eight per cent. Thus, whether an urbanized area is as densely built up as Harlem or as open as Frank Lloyd Wright's Broadacre, the reservation of substantial amounts of additional open space would not materially change the existing environment within the developed sectors. In short, the economic costs of rather large reservations of open space *within* urbanized areas do not seem to be large enough to warrant not taking public action in this direction.[8] These costs are sufficient in most cases to insure that such space will yield to urban use in the private market, for they are likely to be

7. This general point is developed in more detail in *Plan for the Valleys, op. cit.*

8. Assuming maintenance costs are zero, which is the only reasonable assumption, when the use of the land is not specified.

greater than the returns which a private investor could expect from holding the land in an open space use. They do not seem large enough, however, to outweigh the economic costs of developing land which has special value to the community in its natural state.

PUBLIC COSTS OF OPEN SPACE PRESERVATION ARE SIGNIFICANT

Unlike economic costs for society as a whole, which as a rule would appear to be either insignificant or unimportant, public costs associated with the preservation of adequate amounts of open space within, or at the fringes of urbanized areas, could conceivably reach prohibitive levels. As shown in Chapter II, if within the *urbanized* portion of the Philadelphia SMSA, all of the land classified as vital for the maintenance of the water regimen were acquired in fee simple by a public agency, the total cost would be more than $863,000,000.[9] This figure does not include administrative and legal expenses associated with acquisition, tax losses, and annual outlays for maintenance. The capitalized value of these additional costs might well be another $100,000,000. If the land acquisition and subsequent expenses were financed by 40 year, five and one-half per cent, level-payment bonds, the annual interest and amortization charges would total over $59,000,000. Depending on one's point of view, these costs are either huge or quite modest. They certainly are large enough to evoke serious political resistance, unless the benefits of natural open space preservation were more firmly established than has been done here. By contrast, if the same amount of land were acquired well outside the urbanized area, the cost would be only one-fourth or one-fifth as great.

These high figures suggest several points that are very significant

9. This estimate is based on 1962 land prices and hence considerably understates what the cost would be today. See Chapter II, p. 75.

for public policy. First, creation and application of the legal tools discussed in Chapter III, which permit open space preservation without a complete taking of property, would appear to be critical. As already pointed out, these tools must relate specifically to the natural processes which are to be protected.

Second, referring again to Figure 30, if a public agency were the developer in C as well as the preserver in B, it would recoup much of the costs of its open space program as urbanization of land shifted out to C and caused land prices to rise. The agency could not, of course, recover its expenditures simply through higher tax receipts in C, since it would have collected taxes based on urban use in one of the two areas in any event. Clearly, since public bodies today do not have development powers, land prices are a severe restraint on policy alternatives.

Finally, the figures in the illustration raise the very critical question of whether a public body should attempt to acquire land at the fringe, which is more accessible for recreation, but also much more expensive than is land farther out, or whether it should go beyond the fringe for its acquisitions. Assuming in Figure 30 that B is held open and C is developed, if the extra time-distances of crossing B are not really very important, than cannot it also be argued that if B is developed and C remains vacant, the extra time-distance of reaching C from A and B is also not important? One possible answer, though not a wholly satisfactory one, is that to cross B might be burdensome for families living near the center of A, since they already have to go quite far to reach B. Perhaps, therefore, unless the land in B falls into a higher priority classification than C with respect to preservation of natural processes or visual amenities, it makes much more sense in the long run to preserve C, where prices are lower. This question is pursued in somewhat more detail later in the chapter.

ESTABLISHING PRIORITIES FOR PRESERVATION

Even though economic costs of open space preservation appear to be small, given the limited public resources that are available to keep a large quantity of land more or less in its natural state, we are confronted with the question of which acreage to choose. In the past, stated goals of preservation have included conservation of water and other natural resources, flood control, preservation of visual amenity, guidance of urban growth, maintenance and protection of prime agricultural land, and preservation of adequate space for outdoor recreation. The basic premise of this study, however, is that if only those lands which perform essential functions with respect to the water regimen were protected, most of the other open space goals would be served.[10]

Unfortunately, in most urban areas this approach probably will not solve the problem of which lands to preserve. In the Philadelphia SMSA, for example, it turns out that over 60 per cent of the undeveloped portion of the metropolitan area (1,130,000 acres), with an aggregate value of almost one billion dollars, consists of areas that we have classified as being of significance to the water resources system.[11] And, unless all of this land could be brought under control at once, it would be impossible to acquire it for even this huge figure, because the additional demand for such a substantial amount of acreage would cause a significant rise in prices. Equally, comprehensive programs of partial acquisition would also be more expensive. Moreover, if all land of apparent importance to the water regimen

10. These lands are defined in Chapter I.

11. To refresh the reader's memory, there are approximately 2,250,000 acres of land in the PSMSA, of which 1,800,000 were still open when the data for this study were gathered. Approximately 1,130,000 undeveloped acres were identified as being of special value to the water regimen, and 960,000 of these acres were in private ownership. Of the approximately 670,000 lower-priority acres, 635,000 were in private ownership.

were indeed restricted from development, two-fifths of the remaining 635,000 acres of private open land would be urbanized by the year 1985, and over two-thirds would be developed by the year 2000 (assuming, unrealistically, that some of the projected growth did not spill over the SMSA boundary or take place at higher than projected densities). Obviously, quite independent of the political improbability of withholding 60 per cent of the land from use, if preservation efforts actually did succeed, the impact on land prices and on the structure of the metropolis would be both significant and very likely undesirable.

Fortunately, there is no need to bring all of the land under control, for, according to our calculations, if there were no preservation efforts at all, most of the 1,130,000 acres would still be unurbanized in 1985 and in the year 2000. Indeed, a mere one-seventh of the presently unurbanized land in the Philadelphia SMSA will be drawn into urban use by 1985, and only one-quarter will be gone by the end of the century. It should be emphasized that this is the quantity of open land which will disappear either with or without preservation programs. Without such programs, some of the lost acreage will be in the preferred category and some in the unpreferred, whereas with open space programs, primarily the latter land will be developed. On a pure probability basis, therefore, and at the moment there are no data for a more refined estimate, the maximum loss of preferred land will not exceed 25 per cent by the year 2000. This is in part due to the fact that the boundaries of the Philadelphia SMSA lie considerably beyond the edge of the presently urbanized area. Nevertheless, it suggests a much more manageable problem, at least for the area under study.

It also clearly indicates the need for additional criteria in order to establish priorities for partial acquisition and partial preservation. The following discussion examines some of the factors which must be considered in attempting to develop a priority system, and the tentative conclusions which have been reached. There are two analytically different types of priorities which should be kept in mind as the discussion proceeds. The first, priority for preservation, relates to the contribution of the land to open space goals. The second, priority for public action, reflects the relative likelihood of the land being lost to urban use in the absence of changes in public policy.[12]

Contribution to Preserving the Water Regimen

As a first approximation, it would seem that priorities could be partially established on the basis of the aggregate contribution of various types of land to the total set of open space goals. Contributions would be measured by identifying overlapping parameters.[13] For example, other things being equal, land in four preferred categories (say, a forested marsh over an aquifer recharge area and in a flood plain) might be regarded as more critical to the water resource goals than land with three overlaps and so on. Unfortunately, this simplistic view of the measurement problem is quickly destroyed by lack of evidence to support the assumption. No information is available which would permit a ranking of the categories of open land according to their contribution to the water regimen. There is no basis for saying, for example, that land in three categories A, B, and C, should have a higher priority than acreage in two categories, D and E. All that could be assumed with certainty is that other things being equal, ABC

12. This is analogous to the two-step classification of "importance" and "sequence" outlined in Robert Coughlin, "Capital Programming Problem," XXVI, February 1960, pp. 39–48; and in Coughlin and C. A. Pitts, "Capital Programming Process," *Journal of American Institute of Planners,* XXVI, August, 1960, pp. 236–241.

13. In a highly readable discussion of the case for open space, Charles E. Lee suggests a deceptively simple "theory of priority by overlapping functions" (recreation, amenity, and conservation of natural process) which is the same approach originally taken here. Lee, who had access to a draft of the study, brushes aside the problems raised above. See Charles E. Lee, *Challenge of the Land* (New York: Open Space Action Institute, 1967), p. 17.

land should receive a higher rating than AB, BC, or AC acres.[14] But other things are almost by definition not equal, since the marginal contribution of a particular piece of land depends not only on its natural features but also on its location in the metropolitan area.

The overlap approach is, moreover, deficient in failing to include the cost of reproducing the natural process function which a given piece of land performs prior to development. Two types of land may be approximately equal with respect to their contribution to a set of goals, but if both were urbanized, their functions might not be equally inexpensive to replace. Several possible examples could be cited, but again, there are no data to support any ranking of land according to "reproduction" costs.

Finally, and perhaps most important in the Philadelphia situation, even had land been ranked by number of overlaps, very little would have been gained, for in the case of two-thirds of the preferred acreage there are no overlaps at all, and in an additional one-quarter, overlaps of only two categories occurred.

A quite different approach to measuring the relative contribution of various types of open land to the water regimen starts from a conception of the natural resource system as a "seamless web," and postulates that land associated with the system should be held open in all parts of the urbanized area in proportion to the demands which that part of the area places on the system. The web analogy cannot be taken very far, however, since aquifers, marshes, etc. are not equally distributed throughout the region. They have to be preserved where they are. In addition, the approach itself is at present no more measurable than is the one based on the notion of overlapping parameters.

14. The hydrologic models of watersheds now being constructed by Dr. Luna Leopold, Chief Hydrologist of the U.S. Geological Survey, may provide answers to this tricky question.

The concept of a web does, however, suggest three important points: First, inlying open land, though more costly, may also be proportionately more valuable to the natural system since so little of it is left. Conversely, the loss of large amounts of inexpensive farm land may be of little consequence even though this land may fall into one or more preferred categories. Second, in outlying areas where acre zoning predominates, the contribution of private open space to the water system may be so great as to reduce sharply the amount of public intervention needed for this purpose. Last, because of differences in the amount of various types of land already in public or semipublic ownership throughout the region, the goal of proportionality, which is inherent in the web approach, implies different priorities within land-type location categories.

Contribution to Other Open Space Goals (Specifically visual amenity, outdoor recreation and guidance of urban growth)

To the extent that land in one or more preferred categories with respect to the water resource system also performed additional open space functions, it would obviously receive higher priority for preservation. The problem here is that some of the land outside the water-oriented system may perform these functions even better. For example, second-grade farm land is often considerably more scenic than are forested marsh areas. Thus, once additional goals are introduced, all unurbanized land must be reintroduced into the analysis, and the value of the water-oriented classification system in establishing priorities is weakened. Equally important, the measurement problem, which is already formidable, becomes almost impossible when both goals and means become multi-dimensional.

Likelihood of Early Urbanization

With respect to priority for action, one of the obvious key questions is which land is most in danger of beng urbanized in the near future.

Such information should be available in usable form in many of the areas where major transportation studies have been conducted. Assuming these acres can be identified, those which have been given high priority for other reasons might seem to be the ones that should be the immediate focus of public action. However, land which is on the verge of development is high-priced. In addition, preventive action might force development on to other land which has also been assigned a high ranking for open space preservation. Hence, it might make more sense to assign higher priority to land that appears to be on the verge of ripening for urban use (increasing sharply in value), but has not yet done so. Typically, such land is only slightly further removed from the urban edge than is expensive acreage. This question is discussed in somewhat more detail in the next section.

Cost

The question of cost enters the problem of fixing priorities in several ways, some of them immediately apparent, others not. First, assuming that land could be ranked according to its contribution to the water resource system or other open space goals, how would differences in the cost of land among the various categories alter these priorities? To illustrate, the most vitally needed open space might also be the most expensive. Given a fixed sum to spend for acquisition, would it be preferable to preserve a few acres of this land, or many acres of less desired land, or some combination of both? This question becomes academic in the face of the difficulties of ranking the land at all, but if the problem of ranking were solved, existing methods of adjusting priorities to reflect cost differences could be applied.

Second, assuming that all land in the preferred categories were felt to be equally critical to the achievement of open space goals, which locations should receive highest priority for acquisition? The obvious answer would seem to be the cheapest ones. However, since these are well beyond the urban fringe and in no immediate danger of urbanization, areas somewhat less removed would appear to be the logical targets even though they are not the least expensive. This reasoning is supported by the relationship of land prices to distance from the urban core. As has been shown, starting from the center, prices in the Philadelphia SMSA drop rapidly from several hundred thousand dollars per acre to less than $10,000 at about the ten mile ring. Beyond this distance, values begin to taper off more gradually until distance from downtown loses its importance entirely. Near the edge of the urbanized area, then, there is a critical intermediate zone within which differences in accessibility to the center are small, but where differences in land prices are quite large. It would appear that maximum gains could be achieved by focusing acquisitions at the outer edge of this zone.

Third, the costs of preservation and the amount of natural resource land which is protected from urbanization will depend on whether public programs on balance are indeed able to preserve high priority acreage or whether their effect is simply to push urbanization from one preferred area onto another. Conceivably, even with a vast program of acquisition and other forms of control, high priority open land could disappear at the same rate as before. Conversely, a small number of strategically placed acquisitions might, by channelling growth in desired directions, be sufficient to protect most of the acreage.

Fourth, not all so-called preferred land may actually make a substantial contribution to the water regimen. Or it may have an inexpensive nonspace substitute. If better data showed this to be the case, not only would the estimates of total cost be altered but priorities as well.

Finally, as has been said before, since outright acquisition is the most expensive approach, it almost certainly could not be used by itself to implement a large-scale, open space system. Success will probably depend, therefore, on the development of compensable and non-compensable regulations associated with the relative contribution of various types of land to the water regimen as discussed in Chapter III.

ALTERNATIVE APPROACH TO SETTING PRIORITIES

The exercise of trying to establish priorities furnished convincing evidence not only that necessary information was lacking, but more important that with respect to the water resource goals, though not the amenity and recreation goals, the problem was being incorrectly defined. No set of priorities would translate the inventory of preferred natural resource land into a system of open space because our concept of a system was limited. We had created a dichotomy between open and urbanized space which implied either complete preservation or complete development. From the standpoint of the water resource system, however, a certain amount of urbanization should be acceptable everywhere except on flood plains. And, given certain conditions, even flood plains can receive development.

Following this logic, a set of somewhat arbitrary (in that they are untested except by empiric observation) residential density standards that reflect the extent to which different kinds of acreage can be developed without adversely affecting the water regimen, was constructed for various categories of land.[15] Applying these standards, it was calculated that the lands in the preferred natural resource categories alone could absorb at least 700,000 dwelling units if all such units were in low-rise[16] structures, and considerably more if an appreciable number of structures were high-rise. Assuming residential and other kinds of development would occur on both preferred as well as other lands and in the form of in-filling in already built-up neigh-

15. See p. 43.
16. This calculation simply uses the proposed densities for each category.

borhoods, the residential "capacity" of the Philadelphia SMSA even after the imposition of controls would, therefore, be well in excess of projected construction over the next four decades.

With this optimistic conclusion, some caveats should be mentioned. First, to repeat, the standards are arbitrary and open to question and testing. Second, the standards have not been tested spatially to see to what extent they would, if applied, distort projected growth patterns.[17] Third, the public costs of applying the standards have not been estimated. Some of the densities are so low as to necessitate partial compensation to owners and, depending upon the configuration of development, might result in higher costs for public facilities. Fourth, the standards do not necessarily yield a desirable pattern of urbanization. In the absence of additional controls, a continuation of urban sprawl could occur at least as easily as clustering. Fifth, the fiscal consequences to separate governments have not been calculated. Sixth, though this is implied in what has already been said, the whole approach is such that only one of many important variables is being maximized. If only intuitively, attention must be given to other planning considerations. Seventh, the political cost of partial expropriation of a very large number of acres may prove to be greater than complete acquisition of a far smaller number.

Finally, and this too has already been implied, the pattern which is achieved is not an open space system in the conventional sense, but rather a method to protect certain natural processes. The problems of meeting recreational requirements, protecting visual amenities, and providing criteria for guiding urban growth remain. The "system" does, however, provide a good foundation for considering these next steps.

17. See p. 181 for a discussion of the proposed method for testing.

SUMMARY AND CONCLUSIONS

This analysis began in the hope, and possibly the naivete, that: (1) a presumption in favor of preserving more natural beauty within metropolitan areas could be established by demonstrating the insignificance of economic costs of preservation and the potential insignificance of public costs; and (2) the basis for establishing preservation priorities could be created out of empirical data on the price, location, ownership, and natural-resource characteristics of various types of undeveloped land.

Although the analysis has not produced firm guidelines regarding urban forms and program strategies which would inexpensively interlard open and developed space, it does suggest that several forms which have been suggested elsewhere in the literature to halt urban sprawl and provide more space, e.g., greenbelts and new towns, constitute but a few of a range of solutions, and not necessarily the most appropriate ones. The discussion also suggests that a presumption in favor of larger amounts of open space has considerably more theoretical support than even open space advocates themselves may have believed. On the basis of logic alone, it was shown that economic costs are likely to be quite small. Although this is not a startling finding, it refutes a commonly held view among lay persons that economic costs can be measured with reference to market values.

Public costs are much more difficult to pin down, depending as they do on a variety of factors. In the Philadelphia SMSA, acquisition in fee simple of all land which has been identified as of special significance to the water regimen would cost almost one billion dollars plus tax revenues foregone and the expense of maintenance. This is a prohibitive figure; however, our analysis indicated no necessity for special efforts to preserve much of the land and certainly no compelling reason to acquire it all in fee simple. Very crudely, it seems possible that a well conceived mix of preservation programs could reduce the billion-dollar figure by two-thirds to three-fourths, or even more. A figure of this magnitude would seem to be in the realm of political feasibility.

Thus, both public and economic costs do not appear to constitute a major barrier to open space preservation. Yet preservation programs encounter great funding difficulties. In part, this may be due to the lack of clear preservation priorities, the second focus of this chapter. Were it possible to demonstrate convincingly the importance of certain lands to the water regimen, resistance to public acquisition either in fee or in less-than-fee could possibly be overcome. Lacking hard data on this matter, however, the chapter could only adumbrate the factors to consider in determining how much of which kinds of land to preserve completely or partially, in which areas.

One possible solution to the priority problem is to allow at least some development on all land, a strategy which was discussed briefly at the end of the chapter. While this approach is a good beginning toward a set of controls that would speak to amenity as well as conservation values, it too depends for its strength on better evidence about the natural resource value of various kinds of land. Additionally, it requires political acceptance of new forms of land use control on a broad scale.

One thing is clear. What are desperately needed are in-being land use plans that give more equal weight and more objective consideration to both open space and development requirements. The need for such plans is acute not only in the outer sections of metropolitan areas but also in already developed areas where their absence has polarized interests into two groups: developers, both public and private, who continually seek just a little piece of parkland that surely will not be missed; and nature-lovers who are forced to fight equally hard to protect every last inch of existing space. Neither side can justify its arguments, and existing developed and open spaces wind up as givens, except for an occasional marginal realignment at the fringe or the creation of a vest-pocket park. If those who are on the side of trees and green grass had a rationally determined plan that would protect and, in general terms, distribute a total amount of open acreage, part of the conflict would be resolved. Urban development in the inner-areas could be allowed to consume large amounts of existing open acreage, if simultaneously new space were created nearby. Put differently, an adequate open space plan would not only preserve openness within urbanized areas, but accelerate needed development and redevelopment as well.

In brief, then, the conclusion of the economic analysis is that the critical dimensions of the problem are not primarily economic in character. This is the sort of conclusion which is all too easy to reach in any analysis; that is, that the solutions lie somewhere in another discipline. It is hoped, however, that in the process of arriving at this position, the paper has clarified the issues, not simply avoided them.

5

Design of Metropolitan Open Space Based on Natural Process

WILLIAM H. ROBERTS

This chapter is concerned with the design implications, opportunities and the methods used when planning metropolitan open space on the basis of natural process. While traditional approaches to the location of open space in metropolitan areas have preserved many major stream valleys and areas important to natural process, more often open space has been conceived as a residual to a desired development pattern, or as a formal pattern itself. Design for open space should start with a pattern of open space and limitations for development based on maximum preservation of natural processes and amenity. This pattern can then be progressively modified where necessary to accommodate the demands of metropolitan growth. A method is proposed whereby an understanding of the workings of the natural systems and the impact of development on them will permit the tradeoffs to be made with more complete knowledge of the costs and benefits.

148

Few metropolitan populations enjoy proximity to extensive natural wilderness. Many in fact have an uneasy relationship with their environment and the natural processes around them. Those that see mountains from Main Street or have a prospect of the ocean may identify with their own regional setting, enjoying an intangible quality best illustrated by cities such as Caracas, San Francisco, Denver, Vancouver, Pittsburgh, and Rio de Janiero.

Generally, however, urban populations can only enjoy large scale natural landscape by long trips to the open lands far beyond suburbia. The lucky ones may go to the regional parks disposed about and accessible from the city, but more often these are nonexistent. Philadelphia, as elsewhere, continues to expand into its scenic counties and the large scale landscape disappears. The few new parks acquired adjacent to this and other cities fail to satisfy the increased leisure time demands, nor do they help channel urban growth into desirable patterns. Most of near-in open space in any urban area takes the form of golf courses, cemeteries and institutions unusable by the general public and ultimately susceptible to development.

This chapter addresses itself briefly to the history of metropolitan open space concepts and their relevance to natural process as a central concern. It then outlines a design method whereby metropolitan planners can incorporate McHarg's presumption for nature into their current set of procedures.

THE NATURE OF OPEN SPACE SYSTEMS

The literature of planning is replete with conceptual open space patterns as form makers. Except in the case of the turn-of-the-century "romantic" stream valley park systems, open space designers have been concerned with guiding, containing or separating urban growth, distributing recreation, and/or providing scenic amenity, mostly within the framework of geometric abstractions. These include green-

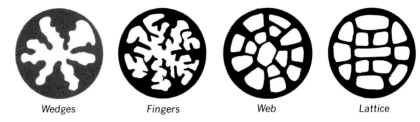

Wedges   *Fingers*   *Web*   *Lattice*

FIG. 31. Compositional concepts of metropolitan open space.

belts, green wedges or fingers, lattices and webs, mats, and rugs.[1] All such compositional concepts are presumed to be perceivable as systems on the ground. That is, if there were changes in parts or elements of the pattern, its interrelated nature would require changes throughout.

This visual sense of a system usually is not realized unless the continuity of the pattern is evident from a continuous natural condition, or linear function. Fairmount Park in Philadelphia can give the observer a sense of structure of such a system because it is related to streams, valleys and ridges and long-distance views. Also, if the open space pattern is linear along an expressway network the various parts may be experienced as connected elements constituting a visual system.

However, the claim of open space to being a "system," in the context of natural process, rests not on geometry, but rather on two relationships. The first is the interrelated character of nature itself and the role of each element and natural condition being significant to the functioning of the system. These must be identified to give the basis for design, and design must devolve from them.

1. See Stanley B. Tankel, "The Importance of Open Space in the Urban Pattern," in *Cities and Space* (Baltimore: The Johns Hopkins University Press, 1963).

The second claim of an open space pattern to being systematic depends on the extent to which it is an element in a larger system whose other elements are the urban pattern.[2]

FORMAL OR COMPOSITIONAL PATTERNS

Formal, compositional and abstract patterns are rarely systematic at large scale: they are historically urban concepts. In one sense they are the simplest illustrations of physical design systems. Yet, whether they are conceived as two dimensional patterns or a sequence of spatial units in some subjective order, and even though they are comprehensible, predictable and man-made on maps, the observer on the ground rarely perceives them.

Ineffective though they are, urban design is still preoccupied by this way of thinking, both for the form of new cities and for the design of regions. Even at the smaller scale, capricious patterns are inappropriate, except where nature is so permissive as to provide a clean slate on which to plan.

Wedges, Fingers, Lattices and Webs

Wedges and fingers are considered first. They are conceived as green fingers between urban corridors radiating from the city center.[3] The idea is to give a structure of open space that relates closely with movement in the city, allows for intermediate linear urban expansion, and makes the open space accessible to the greatest number of people.

The feasibility of wedges or linear parks as a system is determined by regional and local landscape characteristics. It will be extremely appropriate as a system in which the elements coincide with stream valleys, help give richness and legibility to the urban form, and relate to natural resources.

2. See Chapter I, p. 12.
3. See Chapter IV for a discussion of the economic aspects of fingers and greenbelts.

Most regional plans following the Olmsted's lead propose linear parks to be sited along creeks or expressways from the outlying separator belts into the urban core, thus making a thin lattice over the whole metropolitan area.[4] In the early Boston plan of 1901, Charles Eliot proposed wedges where streams and woodlands radiated from the city center outward to the countryside. In Philadelphia, Fairmount Park follows the Schuylkill River and a few of its tributary creeks. This last example is perhaps the finest wedge of those based upon physiographic character. It is large and variable enough to offer great diversity without utilizing too much prime urban land. The steep narrow valleys of its tributaries such as the Wissahickon afford visual enclosure in a surprisingly narrow corridor. As one approaches the city, the park widens to accommodate the various recreation demands of dense central population; and the scale is handsomely transformed from that of a creek to a major river and to vistas of the urban center.

Such a system illustrates the best possibilities of a finger or wedge pattern based upon water, in that its upper reaches have the aspect of wilderness, protect water runoff and can be contiguous with the unurbanized periphery. As the topography becomes less extreme the wider valleys and flat plateaus allow maximum recreational amenity at the area of highest demand.

In another example at a regional scale, *The Plan for the Year 2000,*[5]

4. Frederick Law Olmsted, Sr. and Jr. were authors of many of the stream valley plans throughout the United States in the late 1800s and at the turn of the century.

5. National Capitol Planning Commission, *Plan for the Year 2000* (Washington, D.C.: U.S. Government Printing Office, 1957). See Task Force on the Potomac, *The Potomac,* (Washington, D.C.: U.S. Government Printing Office, 1967) for the conflicts between the proposed urban pattern and natural resource land around Washington, D.C. Washington's earlier open space plan is in fact quite sympathetic to natural resource land. A diagram of this plan appears in Tunnard and Pushkarev's *Man Made America—Chaos or Control,* (New Haven: Yale University Press, 1963), p. 381.

the primary objective is for great wedges of open space and low density housing to force urban development into intermediate and high density corridors along (radial) rapid transit routes. On examination, these radials are in some coincidence with topography and drainage patterns in the northeast through northwest, but they run counter through the rest of the area. Apart from being arbitrary and expensive in these sections, they would also be visually indeterminate because of this conflict with land forms. A plan like this could perhaps achieve some of the growth-directing objectives of a greenbelt, but still allow for linear, controlled expansion. The earlier Copenhagen Regional Plan (1949) is based on the same concept except that there the development corridor is discontinuous and allows for some lateral contact with parks in the radial journey. It is a paradox of these plans that the amount of open space increases as it is further from greatest demand and that lateral connections are neither convenient nor germane to the concepts.

Natural process may be conserved in very large measure by such linear systems as this if they were ever carried out, but it certainly is not the conceptual objective in these examples. They presume nature to exist where development isn't, a fallacy that assumes the abstract intermediate green to be representative of a natural ideal, while the inherent structural pattern of the regional process is neither realized nor utilized in the plan. Even so, they are explicit pointers to the multiple functions that a metropolitan open space system might fulfill, particularly with respect to its influence on urban form.

In another compositional concept, that of lattices or webs, linear ribbons of open space intersect each other in a flexible two-way grid over a metropolitan area. The scale and character of the lattice system would, of course, vary considerably in each region, according to the extent of its application, the interval between the ribbons or corridors, and the criteria upon which the pattern is based. The spacing may be a function of the unique landscape in the region, the particular urban pattern and its population, a desire for physical continuity of park system, or an expressway network as is usually the case.[6]

The highway is a principal place from which people appreciate the national and regional landscape and the collective form of the city. As such, it is an element of the system that physically and psychologically relates the two phenomena of town and country and, at the same time, provides a major recreation activity of millions of Americans. Variable rights-of-way, adjacent linear parks, and sensitive interspersion of the structure into the landscape can bring about an intensified awareness and visual experience to the traveller in motion. In metropolitan regions these open spaces serve a dual purpose in the fact that their perception in motion is supplemented by a totally different scale and function for the local community or park user.

Further linear elements to the lattice concept might include other forms of transportation such as railroads and rapid transit lines. It is somewhat remarkable that railroad lines which surely must be the most intensely used environmental corridors into large cities have never been combined with the parkway idea. Land was almost always reserved for rail-serving uses and as a result the railroad right-of-way achieves a greater visual squalor than any other land the commuter sees from his comfortable seat and large picture window. Railroad rights-of-way could be linear parks that provide a pleasurable outlook while in motion and bisect our communities with ribbons of more agreeable open space as conceptually positive elements in a lattice or other system.

A lattice or web system can be a rich assortment of open spaces that utilizes a great number of linear components to effect its conti-

6. J. Douglas Carroll, the eminent transportation planner, has been the principal proponent of lattice or grid expressway plans (rather than radial) presumably to eliminate points of congestion by providing equal access throughout a region.

nuity in every direction and scale. It can often be based very substantially upon natural process conservation. Although its principal objective is to maximize amenity and guide growth, not preserve natural process, one can expect that an open space system based upon the natural processes about surface water will often assume a physical structure similar to lattice or web.

Greenbelts

The greenbelt idea is probably the most widely known concept of open space planning in relation to metropolitan areas since Ebenezer Howard's Garden City introduced it in 1896.[7]

This concept has been adopted as a basic element of British planning, and applied with considerable concern for the natural characteristics of the sites. Frederick Gibberd and Peter Shepheard, in designing Harlow and Stevenage, new towns outside London, took great care that soils should be tested to ascertain those that were best for farming, recreation, forests, etc. They advocated that in so far as possible the belt of agricultural land should penetrate the town. Anyone who has visited Harlow, however, sees that the open space dissects the town, is overscaled and breaks down all possibility of collective urban identity.

The English greenbelts have served British planners very effectively for both guiding urban growth and interfusing open space with urbanization. They have "prevented the uneconomic exploitation of land on the urban periphery and have compelled the use of vacant lots in urban areas where services are available or can be extended economically . . . thus limiting sporadic and ribbon development. . . ."[8] Further, British prime agricultural land is in critically

7. Ebenezer Howard, *Garden Cities of Tomorrow* (London: Faber & Faber, 1946).
8. Daniel R. Mandelcker, *Greenbelts and Urban Growth* (Madison: University of Wisconsin Press, 1962), p. 88.

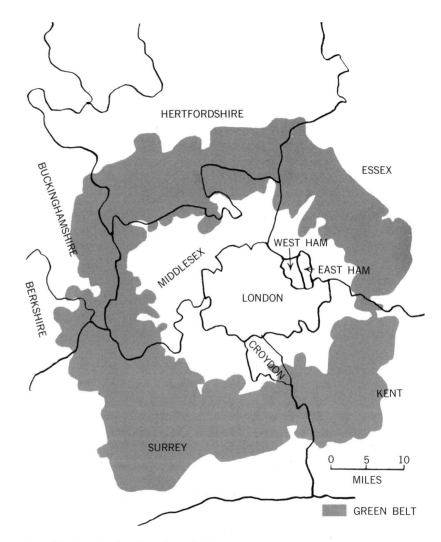

FIG. 32. Greater London Greenbelt.

short supply and the greenbelts are a significant device for conserving it. Six per cent of all English lands is in greenbelts approved formally or in principle.[9]

London's greenbelt is under great pressure for use for development. Where it runs counter to movement patterns and development corridors, it is difficult to maintain. The result has been that one can approach London on an arterial road without experiencing the greenbelt and only see strip development on each side.

If a greenbelt is continuous and sufficiently wide to be an effective barrier it has to cover an arbitrarily large area which is not related to the multiple uses of open space, nor to the differential distribution of natural resources. This latter point is particularly true in those large metropolitan areas that extend over diverse landscape regions, have unequal population distribution, or have strong radial patterns such as transportation or development corridors.

The open space plan for the Baltimore region is a case in point.[10] It proposes two concentric "separator" greenbelts, at about fifteen and thirty miles distance from the urban center, beyond present urbanization in agricultural and wilderness areas. These separator belts follow an intricate pattern to connect the principal reservoirs, valleys and water courses in the region and vary in width from less than half a mile to two or three miles. They terminate at different estuaries along the Chesapeake Bay.

The natural features happen to be remarkably concentric about the urban center of Baltimore and it might be observed that in this unique circumstance natural process conservation would be obtained by belts of connected watersheds, streams, and woodlands as are proposed in the plan. The width of the belts as indicated, however,

9. *Ibid.,* p. 152.

10. Baltimore Regional Planning Council, *Technical Bulletin No. 2,* 1958, pp. 10, 11, and *Open Spaces,* The Council 1959.

may be too small to sustain the conservation role or to provide a discernible interruption to sporadic low-density suburbs. The inherent weakness of the concept seems apparent even in this topographic context. The effective scale and impact of such a belt is minor in spite of its enormous total acreage. It is a minimal visual separator, does not act to control urban growth and form, and is cross grain to the movement and visual experience of a city.

A major weakness of the greenbelt idea thus lies in the fact that it is compositional and intended to contain growth. It cannot allow for the flexibility of the organism it serves. Its conceptual basis is unrelated to any factor of regional natural process.

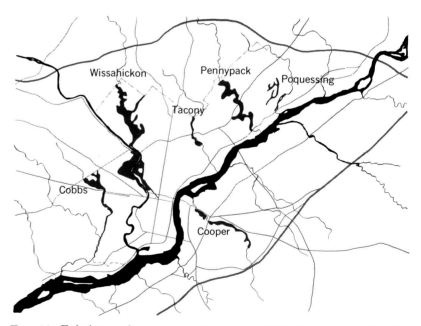

FIG. 33. Existing major stream valley parks: Philadelphia and Camden.

The Pattern of Existing Public Open Space in the PSMSA

The Philadelphia region's present pattern of public open space follows none of these conceptual patterns. It is a composite grab bag of early reservations along rivers and creeks, and scattered parcels of varying size dominated by Fairmount Park and the Wharton Tract.[11]

However, this pattern has little overall relationship to regional natural processes nor does it relate significantly to urban growth. It is the land left over that was too difficult to develop except for the random acts of philanthropists or developers who wanted to foist land they could not use onto the city.

It might be said that in Northeast Philadelphia the city is somewhat belatedly attempting to piece together bits of land "dedicated" by builders into a continuous chain of stream valley parks.[12]

THE GREENBELT AND FINGER CONCEPTS APPLIED TO THE PSMSA

The possibilities for congruence of compositional concepts with the distribution of natural resource land is often high, as indicated in the previous discussion. Ibrahim Jammal[13] illustrates this congruence for the PSMSA by generalizing the pattern into a greenbelt (Figure 34) and nine open space fingers (see Figure 36). These two patterns Grigsby has concluded would have no economic effects of significance, although their fiscal consequences would be great.[14] Jammal suggests that areas common to both plans (Figure 38) might have higher priority

11. See Ch. III, p. 83.

12. See Wallace, McHarg, Roberts, and Todd, *Poquessing Park Plan,* Report to the Fairmount Park Commission, 1968.

13. Ibrahim Jammal, *A Method for Land Range Planning with Application to the Preservation of Open Space in the Philadelphia Metropolitan Area,* unpublished Ph.D. dissertation (in progress). This work is part of a study financed by the Pittsburgh Plate Glass Foundation, 1965–67.

14. See Chapter IV, p. 128.

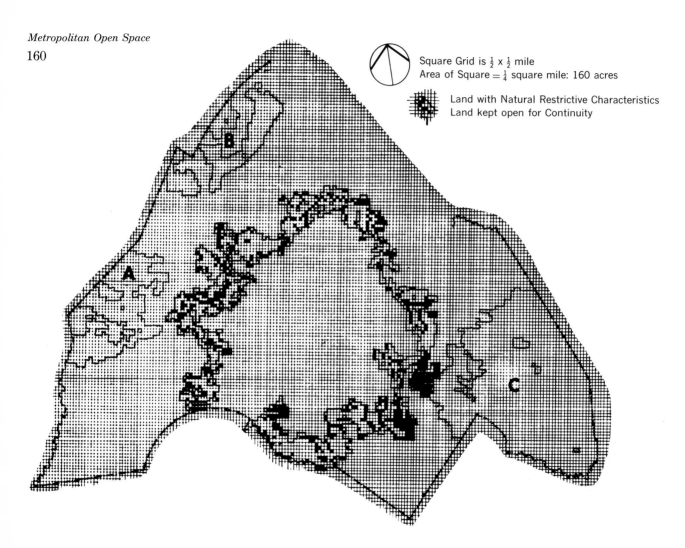

Square Grid is $\frac{1}{2}$ x $\frac{1}{2}$ mile
Area of Square = $\frac{1}{4}$ square mile: 160 acres

Land with Natural Restrictive Characteristics
Land kept open for Continuity

FIG. 34. Hypothetical open space belt plan. PSMSA.

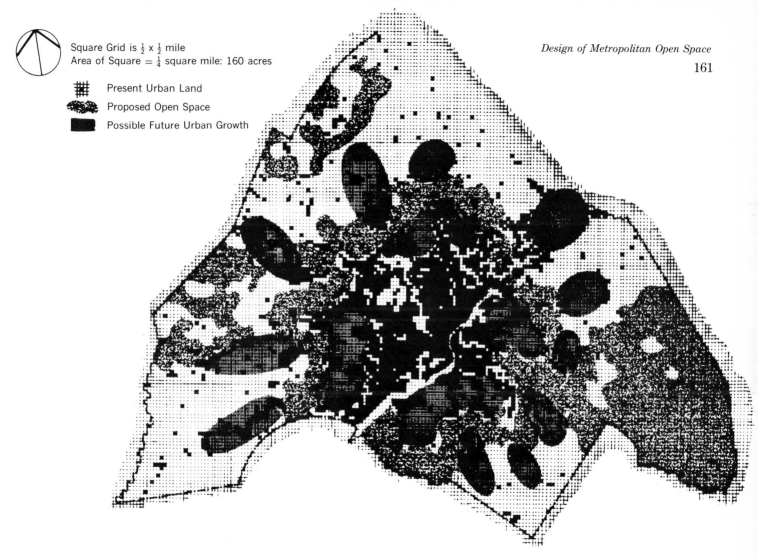

Square Grid is $\frac{1}{2}$ x $\frac{1}{2}$ mile
Area of Square = $\frac{1}{4}$ square mile: 160 acres

Present Urban Land

Proposed Open Space

Possible Future Urban Growth

Fig. 35. Possible future pattern of urban growth with open space belt plan. PSMSA.

of control or acquisition in the process of trade-off with the needs of development.

Jammal describes his method of delineation (*op. cit.,* p. 128): "The two figures represent two generalized future patterns of urban growth and open space. Both these patterns take the existing urban development as a point of departure and assume that it is irreversible. They respect the apparent thrust of development but treat it in two different ways. Both strive to embody the restrictive natural characteristics into configurations of open space that would guide urban growth in different directions while at the same time striving to keep the continuity of natural processes.

"The generalized Finger Plan consists of corridors of open space and corridors of urban land. Urban growth compacts along highways as spines. The fingers are an envelope to the lands that should be kept out of development. The original plan was prepared at the scale of 1 mile = 0.66″; the criteria which determined the shape and location of the O.S. fingers are generalized in the following:

1. Between pairs of apparent corridors of urban development, locate the stream or set of streams (with their surrounding restrictive natural characteristics) which are part of the same watershed.
2. Locate contiguous sets of streams which are parts of other watersheds and which lie between the same pairs of urban corridors considered in (1).
3. Delineate the continuity areas that would connect between the various sets of streams and generalize these sets in an identifiable envelope.

There exist no "rigid" criteria which determine the extent of continuity areas and the exact boundary of the envelope. Although the

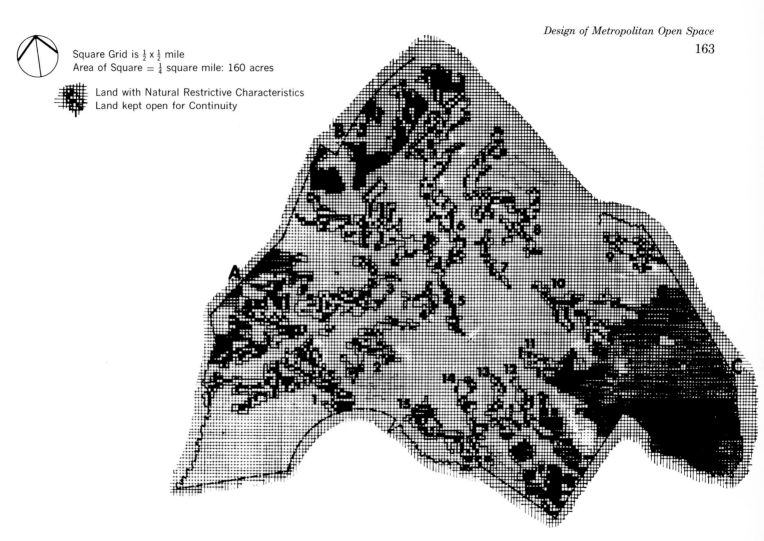

Square Grid is ½ x ½ mile
Area of Square = ¼ square mile: 160 acres

Land with Natural Restrictive Characteristics
Land kept open for Continuity

FIG. 36. Hypothetical open space finger plan. PSMSA.

Square Grid is $\frac{1}{2}$ x $\frac{1}{2}$ mile
Area of Square = $\frac{1}{4}$ square mile: 160 acres

Present Urban Land

Proposed Open Space

Possible Future Urban Growth

FIG. 37. Possible future pattern of urban growth with open space finger plan. PSMSA.

Square Grid is ½ x ½ mile
Area of Square = ¼ square mile: 160 acres

Land with Natural Restrictive Characteristics
Land kept open for Continuity

FIG. 38. Open space areas common to the finger and belt plans. PSMSA.

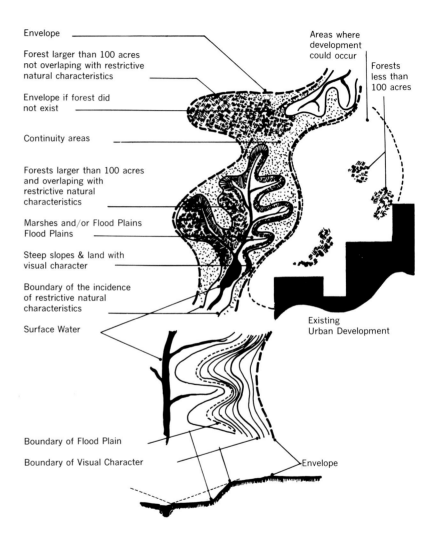

Envelope

Forest larger than 100 acres
not overlaping with restrictive
natural characteristics

Envelope if forest did
not exist

Continuity areas

Forests larger than 100 acres
and overlaping with
restrictive natural
characteristics

Marshes and/or Flood Plains
Flood Plains

Steep slopes & land with
visual character

Boundary of the incidence
of restrictive natural
characteristics

Surface Water

Areas where
development
could occur

Forests
less than
100 acres

Existing
Urban Development

Boundary of Flood Plain

Boundary of Visual Character

Envelope

Fig. 39. Method of delineating the areas to be preserved for open space.

decisions pertaining to their delineation did depend somewhat on the judgment of the planner, those decisions are not totally arbitrary.

"As was pointed out previously, the boundary of the natural restrictive characteristics were adjusted to include areas of visual character; the latter being the steeper walls of the stream valley wherever discernible. Continuity areas around the stream valley would be bound from the stream side by the line of visual character and/or natural characteristics, and from the other side by the plan boundary line.

"The boundary line corresponds as closely as possible to the contour line dividing the flat plateau from the sloping land where the surface watershed of the stream begins. Continuity areas which link two or more watersheds together, to form the O.S. finger, would depend on the existence of intervening urban development, large bodies of forest and/or the minimum area which the planner judges as sufficient to make an adequate continuous link to produce the identifiable open space finger."

The delineation of the Greenbelt Plan was a similar process.

THE DESIGN PROCESS WITH A PRESUMPTION FOR NATURE

The procedure of identifying the physiographic characteristics of an area and understanding the role they play in natural process outlined in earlier chapters is necessary as the basis for an open space pattern or system. This system will help maintain the balance of nature, provide regional recreation as one of its major uses, and go far toward enhancing the urban fabric with an interfusion of amenity.

However necessary, the procedure of identification is not sufficient and is only the first step in a planning and design process. It has been found in application that particular compositional patterns with urban form objectives as discussed are not precluded but may be reinforced by the natural open space network thus revealed.

The concern here is how to combine the procedure with its principles and methods into a metropolitan planning process that takes into account socio-economic and cultural needs as well as natural process. How relatively restrictive or determinant on urban growth will valuing nature and natural process be? Does it dictate, suggest, or merely whisper? Can other goals be satisfied as well, and how should conflicts be handled? In fact, what sort of open space system results and is it a desirable one in relation to urban growth and amenity? How does it compare with previous concepts of metropolitan open space?

What follows is a description of such a design process. It was first developed and tested in the *Plan for the Valleys*[15] and further refined as part of several graduate planning exercises (unpublished) at the University of Pennsylvania's Departments of City and Regional Planning and Landscape Architecture.

The design process starts with the presumption of an open space pattern identified as described in Chapter I. Growth patterns are then forecast and are compared to the open space pattern. In many places they are in conflict, in others they are not. In the examples it was found that much growth could be diverted to those areas not part of the open space pattern by modifying zoning, sewer and highway plans. By a series of steps called "testing," the pattern was evolved that met planning standards, metropolitan form concepts, and preserved amenity to an unusually high degree. Starting with the open space pattern, and subsequently modifying it progressively where necessary to accommodate the growth needs of a metropolitan area is what is meant by "testing."

The term design is used, therefore, in a broad sense to include all the various steps in the process of developing an open space pattern

15. Wallace, McHarg Associates, *op. cit.* (later Wallace, McHarg, Roberts and Todd-WMRT).

and its development corollary into a metropolitan plan. It is not limited to traditional landscape architectural or planning activity.

The total process can be thought of as divided into four major activities. These are called identification of the natural characteristics, testing, optimizing, and landscape design. They are outlined here in a somewhat formalized way as a recommended work program that never loses sight of the presumption that the burden of proof for development of natural resource lands should be on the developers and on the urgency of other socio-economic goals.

Identification of Natural Characteristics[16]

This activity involves going through the steps outlined in early sections of this study. Natural factors will vary both in type and significance in different regions of the country. At one extreme, a metropolis on the plains may find nature relatively permissive and subtle and only suggestive, with climatic and sub-surface factors dominating. Under such conditions man must create an amenity nature has not provided, with tree planting, landscaping, mounding, etc. At the other extreme nature dictates, is vigorously determinant, and must be deferred to. Pittsburgh's plan for example, is rigorously prescribed by the character of hills, valleys and rivers and by natural process at work.[17] The PSMSA is an example in between these two extremes.

In addition to the discrete physiographic elements, areas of unique

16. This first step is similar to that described by Zisman, *op. cit.* pp. 59–60. However, he describes the process of combining the schematic open space pattern with the normal steps of comprehensive planning in only a general way, and does not address himself to the key steps of "testing," during which the presumption for nature is inevitably under constant attack.

17. See David A. Wallace, *Oakland and the Golden Triangle . . . A Conceptual Critique,* Pittsburgh Regional Planning Association, May, 1961.

visual personality should be identified and mapped.[18] These can be considered as "landscape rooms," with floors and walls and the sky for a ceiling. Vernacular exists in landscape architecture, geography and geology to describe them. This language can be combined into a tool for an "image of the country."[19] Such terms as "genius loci" and "landscape identity" are given specific meaning and usefulness.

Parallel with identifying natural characteristics, cultural characteristics of special historic, functional, or symbolic significance should be classified and mapped. This will establish the "path of man"—the things that are meaningful to him. Where these things coincide with the natural phenomena and areas of unique visual personality, "corridors" can be identified of importance to the ultimate plan.[20]

Once the above factors are identified and evaluated for significance, principles similar to those outlined in this study but based on special local characteristics can be developed.[21] They will establish the relative permissiveness or prohibition to development for each type of area. The areas of differing degrees of permissiveness can then be mapped, much as one maps different districts for zoning. The areas thus mapped can be matched against the most suitable uses—those uses that disturb natural processes, the water regimen and other valued elements the least.

Where more than one natural characteristic is present, the more restrictive control would apply,[22] but all of these restraints should

18. Such areas as major valleys whose every part is visible from every other part. See *Plan for the Valleys, op. cit.* for an example of this determination.

19. The "image of the country" could be as useful as the "Image of the City" developed by Kevin Lynch.

20. See Wisconsin, *op. cit.,* for a description of such corridors at a statewide scale.

21. "Significance" in this context means the extent to which the various publics as clients of planning attribute value to the factors and are prepared to take actions to preserve these values.

22. See Chapter III, p. 121.

be addressed with reference to the whole system of natural process over the region and not for any isolate parcel of land.

The Testing Phase: A Successive Accommodation to Goals of Comprehensive Planning

The testing (and optimizing phase) is to determine the degree to which the open space system is consistent or in conflict with other regional and local planning goals, to see where progressive modifications are necessary or new constraints should be anticipated, and examine the relative conflicts inherent in the presumption for nature against the many other objectives and means for implementation of comprehensive planning. The phase involves successive comparisons with the requirements of other goals.

The testing phase falls into seven distinct activities. The first is called a "Structure Test" to evaluate the size, shape, and relationship of proposed development areas. Do such areas correspond to reasonable concepts of community size and structure; is a hierarachal order of places and images evident or possible; does the pattern allow flexibility for changing growth rates, processes and patterns; is there a demonstrable relationship to regional, megalopolis or other urban growth concepts?

An application of the Structure Test to part of the PSMSA's Chester Valley serves to illustrate the method. Having mapped the desirable open space system of natural resource lands as it relates to both natural and cultural determinants, the designer can evaluate the alternate structural patterns that urbanization might take. The first would assume the balance of land after conservation to be uniformly developed so that it accommodates a projected market of normally expected growth. This may be done with the same net density as market forecasts and present zoning might project, or on the other hand, as increased densities to allow for high premiums on

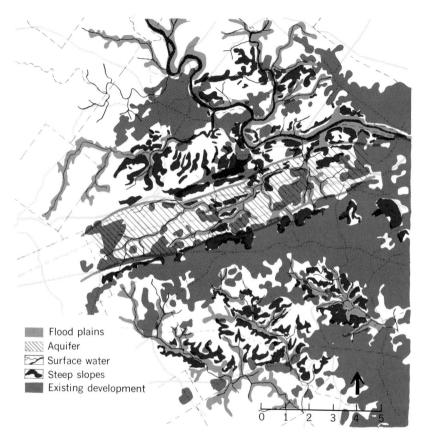

Flood plains
Aquifer
Surface water
Steep slopes
Existing development

0 1 2 3 4 5

Fig. 40. Existing development and natural resource lands—the Chester Valley. PSMSA.

land with greater amenity, more efficient services, and to take into consideration that the large-lot market can be adequately provided for at low density in the limited development areas of the open space system itself.

Examination shows that this first structural pattern for the East Chester County area used in the example has developable areas of land in irregular units measuring one and one-half to two miles across. The topographic and geological structure disperses the major

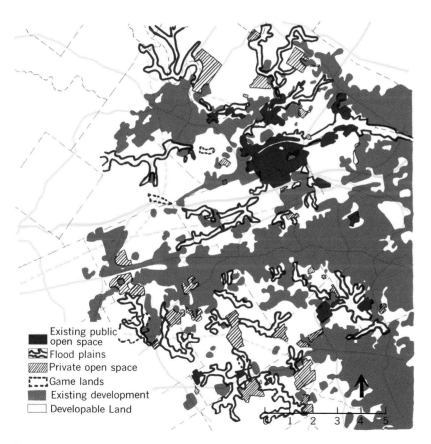

Existing public
open space
Flood plains
Private open space
Game lands
Existing development
Developable Land

0   1   2   3   4   5

FIG. 41. Developable land after flood plain and open space protection—the Chester Valley. PSMSA.

flood plains at about this distance apart, and the main corridors have steep valley walls and are forested. The resulting developable areas have considerable flexibility in size, character, and capacity. The "givens" of institutional lands, distinct landscapes, new lakes, reservoirs and land reserves are "plugged" into the system and various cultural factors are assumed to determine the density and design of development.

This last point is the critical key for the validity of separate structural units of development. If they are assumed to contain the currently typical patterns of tract housing, the open space system serves to steer this development away from areas important to natural process. The open space provides intermediate visual breaks that help define neighborhoods and communities, although no commonality of social and functional needs is necessarily represented. The intermediate breaks would have local and regional recreation and presumably provide for a fringe of low density, higher income housing and institutional uses on the slopes and under forest cover. Compared with existing urban expansion, this pattern would represent a substantial retention of the area's present amenities, and preserve natural resource lands largely in their present state.

Additional benefits of amenity have already been referred to, such as the relationship of transportation to the open space system with "environmental" movement corridors through the region reinforcing and tying the system together.[23] Densities and growth patterns could be directed to take advantage of visual amenity and increased leisure activities with such clarity that both purpose and process were clearly manifest. Furthermore, the growth of each developable unit could be directed to an ultimate density and form that realized social and functional goals of community, hamlet, village, or simply surburbia

23. See p. 153.

or town. As the region becomes developed, a new indigenous urban regionalism which has its own self-maintaining ecology and promises a humane basis for megalopolis can be realized.

The Structure Test applied to the eastern portion of Chester County allows at least three alternative community design concepts consistent with the open space pattern. Each of these pays attention to the distinct landscape regions of the area, the visual uniqueness of the Chester Valley, existing and probable development, planned transportation improvements, a resistant group of land owners, and the limited housing capture-rate at low densities that Chester County can expect from uncontrolled peripheral development in the next 20 years.

The first structure concept would provide separate development areas bounded by a continuous multi-directional open space web. As already mentioned, these may be viable communities of various sizes and natures.

Applied to the study area, this pattern guides and directs the thrust corridors of urbanization. The open space pattern does not pre-empt so much land that the communities are too small or separated,[24] but rather the indication seems to be one of good interfusion of open space into the suburban fabric. Relationship to highways also compares reasonably with the better subdivision and land planning standards. At this scale, however, it is academic to postulate either the transportation or density patterns in greater detail. A significant fact, nevertheless, is that the great Chester Valley is still highly developable under such a concept with good site planning and engineering. The alignment of proposed roads might follow the green web

24. Pockets of very small development would entail inefficiencies of sewerage, streets and community facilities and tend to discourage neighboring and community identity. What the exact signs ought to be must, of course, depend on design below the broad brush level of this analysis.

Urban development
Open space
Existing development

0   1   2   3   4   5

FIG. 42. Structural alternative 1, applied to the Chester Valley. PSMSA.

thus providing extra conservation along the streams by the right of way, a finer highway experience and still a good relationship to the development areas.

The second concept is a variation of the first in that it specifically recognizes the importance of the Chester Valley with its great inter-

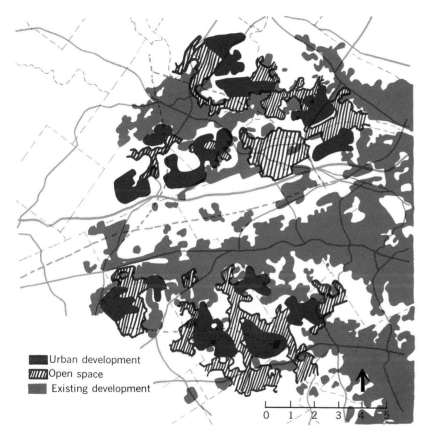

Fig. 43. Structural alternative 2, applied to the Chester Valley. PSMSA.

visibility and its value as prime agricultural land.[25] This fifty mile valley is the most outstanding topographic feature in the county. It is a distinct landscape region, clearly structured, and divides the

25. See Chapter I.

county into two nearly equal parts. It has no major stream, but was formed by the solution and erosion of easily weathered limestones. Ground water yield is variable. Expert opinion[26] has indicated that the nature of soils and geologic structure make its underlying aquifer highly susceptible to pollution over extensive areas. On this basis, and if the retention of valuable scenic and agricultural resources are valued highly the second alternative proposes the Valley to be prohibited from intensive development and preserved for agricultural, large estate and institutional uses.

Contrary to the principles suggested above, current plans conceive the Valley as a major transportation corridor from Philadelphia to central Pennsylvania with development throughout. The proposed Chester Valley Expressway, arterial roads, and a rapid transit system are geared to effect maximum industrial and residential growth along its length and breadth. Present zoning over the aquifer allows extensive industrial areas, some commercial and small lot residential uses. Ironically, the current holding zone of two acre lots can be most damaging to underground water because it would allow on-site (septic tank) sanitary systems. The second concept above proposes intensified development on the higher ground in the manner of hillside and plateau towns or villages. These would overlook and enjoy the Great Valley and be approached by transeptal transportation routes from a regional "parkway" on the valley floor.

A third concept acknowledges that certain inevitabilities such as need for immediate and immense water resource, or maximum accessibility make it absolutely necessary to develop on the valley floor. Alternative ways of going about this might minimize the visual and natural resource damage that might result. First, low intensity devel-

26. See *Natural Environment and Planning*—Chester County Planning Commission, undated.

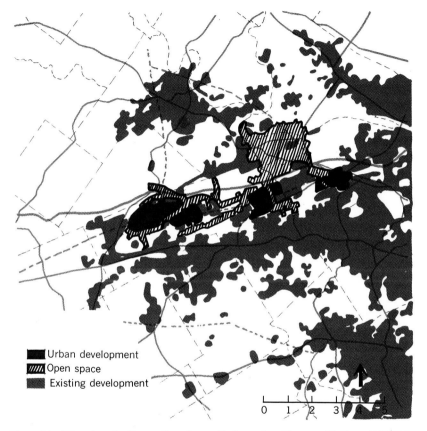

FIG. 44. Structural alternative 3, applied to the Chester Valley. PSMSA.

opment could occupy all of the most suitable lands. The uses might include industries that are not extractive, toxic or pollutant producing, and which cover or disturb only a small proportion of their large holdings. Golf Clubs, colleges, hospitals, cultural areas, estates, and regional parks could be distributed away from the parkway and most critical parts of the natural resource lands, because, these streams, flood plains and sink holes are most susceptible to pollution even if the area is sewered. The valley could accommodate the most desirable regional and local land uses if careful siting were exercised. Residential areas still should be on the higher land as already described in the previous concept. Second, it could also perhaps be proven by detailed testing of soils and substrata that a few locations on the aquifer would safely accommodate intense urban development if that were ultimately marketable. A linear town form might be appropriate. It could be built at very high density and have mass transit connection to the low density residential satellite communities on the adjacent hills, and to the major urban center.

It is evident that planning with a presumption for nature clearly does not inhibit aspirations for structural concepts in regional and urban design, but rather is a system from which variable intrinsic form can be found.

The remaining six design tests are not elaborated to the same degree as the first. They are dependent upon more detailed knowledge of the study area and are listed hereafter.

A "Communications Test" refers to an analysis of existing and proposed highway and rail connections so that the conflict and congruence with the open space system may be observed. Conflict will arise when a route coincides too closely with vulnerable nature characteristics causing their disappearance or damage; for example, in the case of an expressway along a stream bed, necessitating vegetation to be cleared, artificial banks erected against erosion and a culvert built to carry the water. Substantial earth movement and filling associated with expedient alignments also cause great havoc by changing the water table, filling flood plains and marshes, clearing forested slopes and bisecting watersheds. Conflict will also arise with reference to access to the public areas of the open space system, and to the proposed development areas. However, the dynamic linear systems of transportation and open space can each reinforce the expression of the other and coexist as regional design determinants.[27]

A "Development Capacity Test" has three stages. The first is concerned with projections of regional demand for residential units of all types by income and other categories. The gross area of land needed to accommodate this market is then computed on the basis of average net density for each development type. The second stage assigns proportions of this projected growth to various sectors of the metropolitan area according to existing and probable development thrust.[28] The third stage compares the assigned growth to the capacity of the developable areas of the chosen sectors and by this assumption determines how much change may be required in housing-type preference and development density patterns in order for it to "fit." This analysis is necessarily on a metropolitan scale and is the basis for a projected growth process. Recreation requirements and institutional and industrial needs must also be assigned and the patterns tested. In the experience cited, little modification of types or preferences were necessary.

A "Municipal Services Test" examines the feasibility of serving the new growth with an efficient and economical water and sewer system. The system likely under controlled growth can be compared to alternate systems under different growth patterns both for staging and

27. For examples of detailed analysis, see *Plan for the Valleys, op. cit.;* WMRT, *The Least Social Cost Corridor for Richmond Parkway,* Park Dept. of New York, May 6, 1968; WMRT, *A Comprehensive Highway Route Selection Applied to I-95 between the Delaware and Raritan Rivers, New Jersey,* The Delaware-Raritan Committee on I-95, Feb. 8, 1965.

28. See Morton Hoffman, *Baltimore Regional Housing Market Analysis,* Baltimore Regional Planning Council, 1962. This work was the basis for applying the test in the *Plan for the Valleys.*

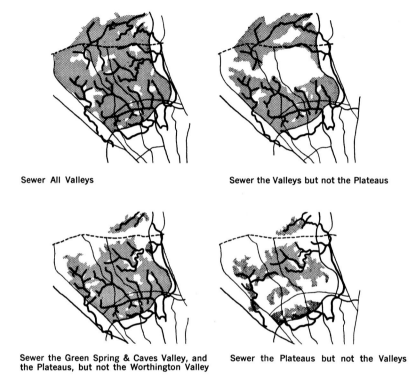

Sewer All Valleys   Sewer the Valleys but not the Plateaus

Sewer the Green Spring & Caves Valley, and   Sewer the Plateaus but not the Valleys
the Plateaus, but not the Worthington Valley

FIG. 45. Alternate sewer alignments, in *Plan for the Valleys*.

capacity. It should be observed that public policy with regard to municipal services is a primary determinant of regional urban growth. Development can be discouraged or encouraged at various densities according to the presence, staging or absence of these facilities. Planning municipal services should be a conceptually positive act related to regional planning goals; they are the third linear dynamic system that can work in conjunction with the multiple benefits of natural

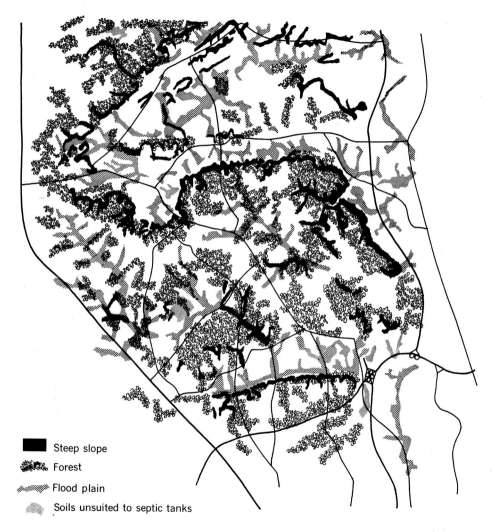

FIG. 46. Natural features Green Spring and Worthington Valleys of Maryland.

process system planning. Figure 45 illustrates the basis of comparison developed for the *Plan for the Valleys*.

Additional tests are for implementability and congruence with social goals. Implementation requires a series of progressive and accumulating controls which over time effect the realization of the plan by public and private action.[29] It should be anticipated that as new and original design concepts are market tested and acknowledged to be in the common interest, new implementation devices will be developed. A test for social goals might analyze the social implications of open space constraints and community structure and size as they affect political and community purpose. This is an activity which identifies the local and regional problems and aspirations of the population as affected by planning.

The design implications of planning with a presumption for nature are both numerous and exciting. Essentially, it is a multi-purpose approach for conserving indispensable natural resources. Societal values are implicit and must be explicated so that alternatives can be adequately weighed.

The Optimizing Phase: The Trade-offs in Comprehensive Planning

Anticipated growth models developed in a time sequence can form the basis for optimizing.[30] Start with a first five-year sequence which probably cannot be influenced very much. All those controls immediately feasible of application can be instituted, particularly in areas

---

29. See Chapter III.

30. Optimizing is used loosely rather than in a strict economic sense. Optimum here means that combination levels of satisfaction of various goals which aggregates to the most total satisfaction. When goals are in conflict, optimizing is the process of mediating between their demands. It is recognized that real optimization can only be done by rigorous mathematical methods and the present process is in this sense sub-optimization. However, it is a necessary prelude to assigning numerical weights to more sophisticated techniques.

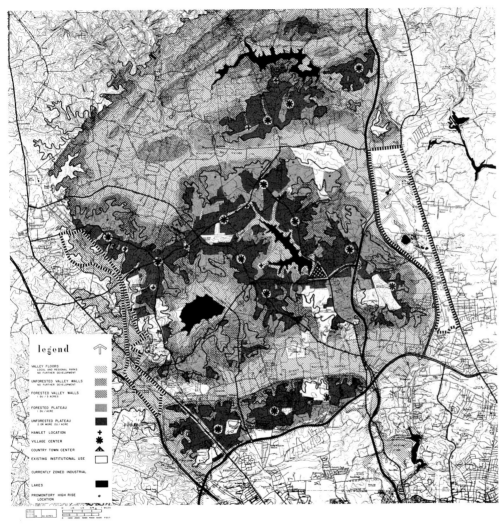

FIG. 47. Optimum land use, in *Plan for the Valleys.*

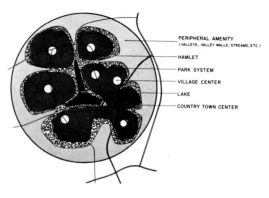

PERIPHERAL AMENITY
(VALLEYS, VALLEY WALLS, STREAMS, ETC.)

HAMLET

PARK SYSTEM

VILLAGE CENTER

LAKE

COUNTRY TOWN CENTER

FIG. 48. Country town and village concept, in *Plan for the Valleys.*

where there is the greatest likelihood of early development. Proposed public works should be examined. Where possible, sewer and highway extensions should be used to guide growth, rather than respond to it, perhaps at the expense of less efficient use of them in early years.

The optimizing process uses the same basic conceptual method employed in the Penn-Jersey Transportation Study,[31] but includes open space as an additional element (along with the traditional transportation and development elements), in the sequential analysis of the impact of each on the other.

The result is a planned growth model, which recognizes that in the early phases, much of the desirable open space pattern may be lost, but with progressive addition of stronger controls the later years of development can be guided more and more toward the preservation of natural resource lands.

31. See Henry Fagin, "The Penn-Jersey Transportation Study," *Journal of the American Institute of Planners,* Vol. 29, February 1963, pp. 9–18.

The final step in the design process recognizes that the results of the previous steps are, again, necessary *but not sufficient* to creating an environment that protects natural process, preserves amenity, and accommodates development. The designer has, in effect, been painting with a broad brush, and must get to the detailed level of site planning at the micro-scale with a continued concern for the presumption for nature.

At the level of detail of subdivision, village, and highway design, greater refinement and creative modification is necessary. Forestation, development of lakes, creation or blocking of vistas, protection and treatment of slopes, all have their role in the final product, and must be skillfully designed to create a humane environment or much of the value of the macro-design process will be negated, and the results will be unsatisfactory. The significant thing is that by following the processes and methods outlined previously, the landscape designer will start with a meaningful program and a basis for intrinsic form which will make his contribution creatively significant in the larger context. The architect and engineers at the micro-scale will also be able to

Fig. 49. Forested valley walls (development at one house for each three acres).

discover similar perceptions for their work and make it relevant to the larger systems.[32]

THE NEW REGIONALISM

The patterns and systems for open space conceived by generations of planners and designers are perhaps "false alternatives" to the conservation of the larger green matrix as Mumford suggests. But they also express the frustrations of the long and perplexing search for "determinants" for a fundamental system that conserves wilderness about the city, directs the growth of urbanization and brings nature into the daily experience of city men, women, and children.

Part of this frustration is possibly due to the dichotomy between the functions and need of open land adjacent to and about cities, and the open land within the built-city fabric. These two needs have been motivated by different cultural aspirations. It has rarely been recognized that the parameter common to both is the unique character of place which nature manifests—the landscape identity, the genus loci.

It may follow therefore, that with insights for natural processes that sustain and enhance man's environment, designers will evoke planning and design solutions that are intrinsic and amenable to each place. An ecological basis for design is necessarily regional. When it is properly understood, the uniqueness of each place and part of a metropolitan area or megalopolis can be manifested in land planning and landscape architecture.

32. See WMRT, *Open Land Study* (for Cylburn Town), Baltimore Department of Planning, 1968, as an example of the follow through necessary to the new approach.

FIG. 50. The Green Spring and Worthington Valleys of Maryland. (The Baltimore Beltway is in the foreground.)

Appendix:
Methodology for Chapter II

DETERMINATION OF LAND VALUES

The determination of land values started by adopting the municipality as a unit of analysis. This procedure necessitated compiling data on values for close to 300 municipalities in seven suburban counties. Philadelphia was excluded since it no longer has open lands free from the direct and immediate impact of urbanization. For most municipalities, it was possible to obtain data on the average value per acre of land as estimated by assessors for purposes of taxation. Usually such information is reported without separating the value of improvements and any value computed without such separation will be seriously distorted. In the case of the three New Jersey counties and Bucks County in Pennsylvania, it was possible to obtain data on the value of open lands as distinguished from land with improvements. For the remaining three counties, the same information was computed by utilizing as independent variables the percentage of urban lands in each municipality; the ratio of population to urban land; the airline distance from downtown Philadelphia; and the total value per acre of land and improvements. The dependent variable was the value of land without improvements. The coefficients were derived by applying the formula to a large sample of the municipalities for which the dependent variable was known.

The average market values available for each of the municipalities were used as a base from which to start a more detailed investigation. These values were plotted on a map of the metropolitan region and an isovalue pattern was depicted, connecting all points (the geographic centers of municipalities) of equal values and fixing in a more appropriate way, zones in which the average value of open land is approximately the same. Isovalue lines were drawn representing values ranging from $50 to $7,500 per acre. The other values plotted were $100; $250; $500; $1,000; $1,500; $2,000; $3,000; $4,000; $5,000; and $6,000 per acre of open land.

The next step was to check on the validity of the isovalue lines. It began first by accumulating data on recent sale prices from transactions dating from 1961 through 1963. Each transaction was identified on the map and after a fairly representative sample was accumulated, these prices were related to the pattern of iso-values. Some discrepancies were found and the iso-value map was adjusted accordingly. Transactions were ignored if there was clear evidence that the site being transferred was primarily a vacant city lot that did not qualify any longer for our open space classification or occurred at a major highway intersection. Our interest being primarily in major tracts of unsubdivided lands, the isovalue map reflects only the value of such lands.

Most of the sales that were used to check the isovalues were in the part of the metropolitan area undergoing rapid change in land use. Therefore, it became clear that a further check on the validity of the map was still essential. This was accomplished by a field survey. Twenty-one municipalities were selected, three in each of the seven counties, for the field check. The selection took into consideration the full coverage of all conditions in each county as well as in the metropolitan area as a whole. In each county, one municipality was selected in the zone where the pressures of urbanization are high, another municipality in the middle part, and the third in the rural outskirts of the county.

The results of the survey led to only minor modifications in the isovalue map for, in general, the values set by the appraisers were in agreement with those already mapped. After the map was readjusted, separate parts, each covering one county, were mailed to the appraisers who checked the validity of the isovalues for their counties.

A final check was accomplished by imposing the isovalues over a map of existing urban lands and major transportation lines. All the peaks in the isovalue map were found to coincide with existing urban clusters and closely followed major highways.

MEASUREMENT OF THE ACREAGE AND VALUE OF OPEN LAND

For empirical purposes, the pattern of the distribution of open lands, the maps of the natural categories, and the isovalue map had to be transformed into figures. To accomplish this objective a technique based on the use of square grids was developed. The Philadelphia Standard Metropolitan Area was subdivided into 14,048 square grids each representing an area of one-quarter square mile. In order to tie the information compiled for this study with that of the Penn-Jersey Transportation Study, it was decided that the grid used by the latter should be adopted.

Within the cordon area, which covers the inner one-third of the region, the Penn-Jersey unadjusted grid coincides exactly with the grids utilized in this study. For areas outside the cordon line, however, Penn-Jersey relies on one square mile grids. In other words, for these areas each Penn-Jersey grid was subdivided into four grids. For purposes of detailed analysis each of the quarter square mile grids utilized as basic units of analysis was further subdivided into four quarters each representing an area of 40 acres.

Each of the basic grids was assigned the same set of coordinates used in the Penn-Jersey grid system. For further identification each grid was coded in relation to its location by county and municipality. In addition, for each grid the airline distance to downtown Philadelphia and the average land value per acre was identified (see Form I).

The measurement of the natural parameters, the urban lands, public lands, and semi-public lands proceeded on two main levels: first, for each of these classifications the occurrence in each of the basic grids was identified in percentages. All figures were rounded to the nearest 10 per cent. This step permitted the calculation of the acreage in each ecological land use category. Second, each quarter grid (40 acres) identified by number, was further coded to indicate whether or not a category exceeded 50 per cent of the total area of the grid.

In addition, basic grids that were surrounded on all four sides by urbanized areas were identified. Following the completion of the data transmission phase, the information compiled was then punched on IBM cards and analysis proceeded.

University of Pennsylvania   Sheet No. <u>1967</u>
Institute for Urban Studies
URA Open Space Demonstration Study

The Philadelphia Standard Metropolitan Statistical Area.
December 1963   Form I

Grid Number						County & Township			Urbanization in adjacent Grids	Urban Lands					
X			Y							% of Grid	Occurrence by ¼ Grids				
1	2	3	4	5	6	7	8	9	10	11	12				
4	9	5	3	7	0	6	2	1		2		1			

Aquifer Recharge					Aquifers					Marshes				
% of Grid	Occurrence by ¼ Grids				% of Grid	Occurrence by ¼ Grids				% of Grid	Occurrence by ¼ Grids			
13	14				15	16				17	18			
8		1	3	4	6			3	4					

Classification form for natural resource characteristics and urbanized area.

Steep Slopes		Forests		Prime Agriculture	
% of Grid	Occurrence by ¼ Grids	% of Grid	Occurrence by ¼ Grids	% of Grid	Occurrence by ¼ Grids
19	20	21	22	23	24

Flood Plains		Surface Water		Restricted Lands	
% of Grid	Occurrence by ¼ Grids	% of Grid	Occurrence by ¼ Grids	% of Grid	Occurrence by ¼ Grids
25	26	27	28	29	30
				3	4

Distance		Average Value				Ratio		Land Value per acre				Tax Rate		Tax Base $(000)					
31	32	X	X	X	X	X	X	33	34	35	36	37	38	39	40	41	42	43	44
2	1	2	0	0	0														

Credits

Frontispiece. Aero Service Division, Litton Industries
  2. Skyviews
  6. Ian L. McHarg
  7. Ian L. McHarg
13. Wallace, McHarg, Roberts and Todd (WMRT)
14. Ian L. McHarg
15. Grant Heilman
24. WMRT
25. Arthur F. Fawcett, U.S. Department of the Interior, National Park Service.
26. Aero Service Division, Litton Industries.
27. Grant Heilman
28. Dr. Jack McCormick
34. I. Jammal
35. I. Jammal
36. I. Jammal
37. I. Jammal
38. I. Jammal
39. I. Jammal
45. WMRT
46. WMRT
47. WMRT
48. WMRT
49. WMRT
50. WMRT

Referential Bibliography

BALTIMORE REGIONAL PLANNING COUNCIL. *Open Spaces.* Technical Report No. 5. Baltimore: State Planning Department, 1960.

——. Standards for Parks, Recreation Areas, and Open Spaces. Technical Report No. 2. Baltimore: State Planning Commission, 1958.

BURTON, IAN. *Types of Agricultural Occupancy of Flood Plains in the U.S.A.* University of Chicago Department of Geography Research Paper No. 75, 1962.

CHAPIN, STUART F., JR. *Urban Land Use Planning.* Urbana: University of Illinois, 1965.

CHESTER COUNTY PLANNING COMMISSION. *Chester County: Natural Environment and Planning.* West Chester, Pennsylvania, 1963.

CLAWSON, MARION, and STEWART, CHARLES. *Land Use Information: A Critical Survey of U.S. Statistics Including Possibilities for Greater Uniformity.* Baltimore: Johns Hopkins Press, 1965.

CLAWSON, MARION. "Land Use and Demand for Land in the

United States," in *Modern Land Policy.* [Papers of the Land Economics Institute, University of Illinois, Harold G. Halcrow *et al.,* ed.] Urbana: University of Illinois Press, 1960. Pp 12–14.

COUGHLIN, ROBERT. "Capital Programming Problem," *Journal of the American Institute of Planners,* Vol. XXVI, February, 1960.

COUGHLIN, ROBERT and PITTS, C. A. "Capital Programming Process," *Journal of the American Institute of Planners,* Vol. XXVI, August, 1960.

FAGIN, HENRY. "The Penn-Jersey Transportation Study," *Journal of the American Institute of Planners,* Vol. XXIX, February, 1963.

GOTTMAN, JEAN. *Megalopolis.* New York: The Twentieth Century Fund, 1961.

HOWARD, EBENEZER. *Garden Cities of Tomorrow.* London: Faber & Faber, 1946.

HOFFMAN, MORTON. *Baltimore Regional Housing Market Analysis.* Technical Report No. 6. Baltimore Regional Planning Council. Baltimore: State Planning Department, 1962.

INSTITUTE FOR ENVIRONMENTAL STUDIES, Upper East Branch Brandywine Project. "The Plan and Program for The Brandywine." Philadelphia, November, 1968.

JAMMAL, IBRAHIM. A Method for Land Range Planning with Application to the Preservation of Open Space in the Philadelphia Metropolitan Area. Unpublished Ph.D dissertation (in progress).

KATES, C.; WILLIAM, ROBERT; and WHITE, GILBERT F. "Flood Hazard Evaluation," in *Papers on Flood Problems,* Gilbert F. White, ed. University of Chicago, Department of Geography, Research Paper No. 70, 1961.

KATES, C., and WILLIAM, ROBERT. *Hazard and Choice Perception in Flood Plain Management.* University of Chicago, Department of Geography, Research Paper No. 78, 1962.

LEE, CHARLES E. *Challenge of the Land.* New York: Open Space Action Institute, 1967.

LESSINGER, JACK. "The Case for Scatteration," *Journal of the American Institute of Planners,* Vol. XXVII, August 1962, pp. 159–69.

MacKaye, Benton. *The New Exploration: A Philosophy of Regional Planning.* New York: Harcourt Brace & Co., 1928.

Mandelker, Daniel R. *Green Belts and Urban Growth English and Country Planning in Action.* Madison: University of Wisconsin Press, 1962.

McHarg, Ian L. "Processes as Values" in *Design with Nature.* New York: Natural History Press, 1969.

National Capital Planning Commission. *Plan for the Year 2000.* Washington, D.C.: Government Printing Office, 1957.

Odum, E. P. *The Fundamentals of Ecology.* Philadelphia: W. B. Saunders, 1959. Potomac Planning Task Force. *The Potomac; A Report on Its Imperiled Future and a Guide for Its Orderly Development.* Prepared for the Department of the Interior. With Introduction by Secretary of the Interior Stewart L. Udall. Washington, D.C.: 1967.

State of Wisconsin, Department of Resource Development. *Recreation in Wisconsin.* Madison, 1962.

Strong, Ann Louise. *Open Space for Urban America.* Washington, D.C.: Department of Housing and Urban Development, 1965.

——. *Open Space in the Penjerdel Region.* (Pennsylvania–New Jersey–Delaware Metropolitan Project, Inc.). Penjerdel, Philadelphia, 1963.

Tankel, Stanley B. "The Importance of Open Space in the Urban Pattern," in *Cities and Space.* Lowden Wingo, Jr., ed. Baltimore: Johns Hopkins University Press, 1963.

Toulan, Nohad A. *Distribution and Market Values of Open Land in the Philadelphia Standard Metropolitan Area.* Philadelphia: Institute for Urban Studies, University of Pennsylvania.

Toulan, Nohad A. Public and Private Costs of Open Space Preservation, unpublished PhD. dissertation. University of Pennsylvania, 1965.

Tunnard, Christopher, and Pushkarev, Boris, in association with Baker, Geoffray. *Man Made America Chaos or Control.* New Haven: Yale University Press, 1963.

WADLEIGH, CECIL H. "The Application of Agricultural Technology," in *Soil, Water and Suburbia.* U.S. Department of Agriculture and U.S. Department of Housing and Urban Development. Washington, D.C.: U.S. Government Printing Office, 1968, pp. 41–53.

WALLACE, DAVID A. *Oakland and the Golden Triangle . . . A Conceptual Critique.* Pittsburgh Regional Planning Association, May, 1961.

WALLACE, McHARG ASSOCIATES, *Plan for the Valleys.* Green Spring and Worthington Valley Planning Council Inc., Towson, Maryland, 1963.

WALLACE, McHARG, ROBERTS and TODD. *The Least Social Cost Corridor for Richmond Parkway.* Department of Parks and Recreation, City of New York, May 6, 1968.

———. *An Ecological Study for the Twin Cities Metropolitan Area.* Prepared for the Metropolitan Council of the Twin Cities, 1969, mimeo.

———. *Open Land Study* (for Cylburn Town). Baltimore Department of Planning, 1968.

———. *Poquessing Park Plan.* Report to the Fairmount Park Commission, Philadelphia, 1968.

WHYTE, WILLIAM, JR. "Urban Sprawl" in *Exploding Metropolis.* The Editors of Fortune. New York: Doubleday, 1958.

WITALA, S. W. *Some Aspects of the Effect of Urban and Suburban Development on Runoff.* Lansing, Michigan: U.S. Department of the Interior, Geological Survey, August, 1961.

ZISMAN, S. B. et al., *Where Not To Build: A Guide for Open Space Planning.* Technical Bulletin 1, U.S. Department of the Interior, Bureau of Land Management. Washington, D.C.: U.S. Government Printing Office, April, 1968.